May She Have
a Word with You?

May She Have a Word with You?

Women as Models of How to Live
in the Poems of Charles Wesley
with Commentary

S T Kimbrough, Jr.

FOREWORD BY
Laceye C. Warner

 CASCADE *Books* • Eugene, Oregon

MAY SHE HAVE A WORD WITH YOU?
Women as Models of How to Live in the Poems of Charles Wesley with Commentary

Cascade Books
An Imprint of Wipf and Stock Publishers
199 W. 8th Ave., Suite 3
Eugene, OR 97401

www.wipfandstock.com

PAPERBACK ISBN: 978-1-5326-4805-2
HARDCOVER ISBN: 978-1-5326-4806-9
EBOOK ISBN: 978-1-5326-4807-6

Cataloguing-in-Publication data:

Names: Kimbrough, S. T., 1936–, author. | Warner, Laceye C., foreword.

Title: May she have a word with you? : women as models of how to live in the poems of Charles Wesley with commentary. / S T Kimbrough, Jr. ; foreword by Laceye C. Warner.

Description: Eugene, OR : Cascade Books, 2019. | Includes bibliographical references and index.

Identifiers: ISBN 978-1-5326-4805-2 (paperback) | ISBN 978-1-5326-4806-9 (hardcover) | ISBN 978-1-5326-4807-6 (ebook)

Subjects: LCSH: Wesley, Charles,—1707–1788. | Christian poetry, English—18th century. | Women in Christianity. | Methodist women—England—History—18th century.

Classification: BX8345.7 .K55 2019 (print) | BX8345.7 .K55 (ebook)

Manufactured in the U.S.A.   JULY 9, 2019

A Select List of Some of Charles
Wesley's Poems About Women

Table of Contents

TABLE OF CONTENTS

Foreword

In the pages that follow, the Rev. Dr. Kimbrough offers a treasure of poetry featuring the exemplary lives of eighteenth-century Christian women. Kimbrough, Research Fellow in the Center for Wesleyan Studies at Duke Divinity School, shares his tremendous creative talent through the curation and commentary of this collection. His keen eye, trained by a lifetime of artistic and scholarly achievements, shapes the selection of a unique collection of poetic portraits previously left unattended, in relative obscurity, little known to scholars, much less wider audiences.

The poet, Charles Wesley—a graduate of Oxford, priest, and poet of the eighteenth century—contributed to the founding of the early Methodist renewal movement in the Church of England, and is one whom Kimbrough has studied and written about extensively. While Charles Wesley is well-known among Anglo-Methodist audiences, many of the women in the poetic tributes, particularly those from modest backgrounds, seem not to appear in any other historical materials. Fortunately, the poetry of Charles Wesley, among other primary sources, is recently accessible through online sources (The Center for Wesleyan Studies at Duke University Divinity School).

The collection is significant for its historical contribution, namely the acknowledgment of women from a wide variety of social backgrounds—from the very elite to the most humble and unknown. Each poem is included in its entirety, allowing the reader to be immersed in the beautiful and poignant imagery portraying the faithful Christian witness embodied in the lives of these women. Historical commentary, informed by Kimbrough's scholarly attentiveness, is provided throughout, as well as a thorough bibliography of complementary material.

This collection is a rare gift of interdisciplinary expertise, reflecting upon the lives of women devoted to their witness of the Christian faith. With gratitude to Wesley and Kimbrough, these women's lives may speak into the imagination of Christian disciples and communities across time and space. May the example of these Christian women and their tributes inspire many—in Charles Wesley's words memorializing his mother, Susanna Wesley:

"In sure and steadfast hope to rise."

Laceye C. Warner
Associate Professor of the Practice of Evangelism
and Methodist Studies
Duke Divinity School
Durham, North Carolina

Abbreviations

AM	*Arminian Magazine.*
CSWT	Center for Studies in the Wesleyan Tradition. There are a number of citations from manuscript versions of Charles Wesley's poetry. These manuscript versions may be found on the *CSWT* website at: http://www.divinity.duke.edu/initiatives-centers/cswt/wesley-texts/manuscript-verse.
FH 1746	*Funeral Hymns.* [London: Strahan, 1746].
FH 1759	*Funeral Hymns.* London: [Strahan], 1759.
HGF 1746	John Lampe. *Hymns on the Great Festivals and Other Occasions.* London: for M. Cooper, 1746.
HSP 1742	*Hymns and Sacred Poems.* Bristol, UK: Farley, 1742.
HSP 1749	*Hymns and Sacred Poems.* 2 vols. Bristol, UK: Farley, 1749.
MM	*Methodist Magazine.*
MS FH	*MS Funeral Hymns (1756–87).* http://divinity.duke.edu/sites/divinity.duke.edu/files/documents/cswt/35_MS_Funeral_Hymns_1756-87.pdf.
MS Journal	*The Manuscript Journal of The Reverend Charles Wesley, M.A.* 2 vols. Edited by S T Kimbrough, Jr. and Kenneth G. C. Newport. Nashville: Abingdon, 2008.
PCWS	*Proceedings of the Charles Wesley Society.* 21 vols. 1994–2017.
PW	*The Poetical Works of John and Charles Wesley.* Edited by George Osborn. 13 vols. London: Wesleyan-Methodist Conference Office, 1868–1872.

| RV | *Representative Verse of Charles Wesley.* Edited by Frank Baker. London: Epworth, 1962. |
| UP | *The Unpublished Poetry of Charles Wesley.* 3 vols. Edited by S T Kimbrough, Jr. and Oliver A. Beckerlegge. Nashville: Abingdon/Kingswood, 1988, 1990, 1992. |

Technical Matters

1. Unless otherwise noted, biblical quotations are from the King James Version of the Bible / Authorized Version, since it was the version generally used by Charles Wesley. Much of the language of his poetry is directly related to the language of that version.

2. All words and phrases that appear in italics in Charles Wesley's verse were italicized at his bidding unless otherwise noted.

3. Where feasible and appropriate, "God's" has replaced the third person masculine possessive pronoun "his" and "God" for the third person accusative pronoun "him."

4. Personal pronouns in reference to God appear in lower case.

5. Some references are to stanzas and line(s) of stanzas, e.g., Part I, 7:3–5, which means Part I, stanza 7, lines 3–5.

6. Since these poems were written by Charles Wesley as tributes or remembrances of the women studied in this volume on the occasion of their deaths, he usually listed the date of their deaths at the beginning of a poem. He is not, however, consistent in this style. Most commonly he listed the month, day, and year. At other times, he states only the month and year, e.g. Miss Francis Cowper (1716–1742). In two instances cited here he gives no date at all, e.g., Mrs. Hannah Dewal

(also Dewell, 1700–1762) Hannah Butts (1720–1762). Wesley did not provide the dates of birth or birth years, which are provided in this paragraph of the women whom he is honoring, but in the instance of two women in this study, one can determine the birth year, since he designated their ages at the time of death, e.g., Mary Horton (1752–1786) and Prudence Box (1740–1778). Dates of the following women have been determined from other sources: Lady Hotham (b. ?1714–1756), Mrs. Lefevre (1723–1756), Mary Horton (1752–1786), and Molly Leyshon (also Leyson, 1721–1750).

7. After the names of the eighteenth-century women at the beginning of each chapter, the death date, if provided by Wesley, has been included. Death dates not included in his manuscripts or publications appear in brackets.

Introduction

Charles Wesley, the distinguished and eloquent poet-priest of the eighteenth century, was born into a family in which the women far outnumbered the men. Early he came under the strong influence of his mother Susanna, whose teaching gifts had lasting effects on his life. She gave birth to nineteen children, but only ten survived infancy, and seven of them were girls. Their impact on Charles's life is clearly reflected in his poetry and letters. For some he was a "brother confessor," and for others more like a good friend. He yearned that they live with Christ and the church at the center of their lives and have wholeness and happiness. He had one sister, Mehetabel or Hetty, who possessed particularly keen intellectual ability, was a fine poet, and could read the Greek New Testament when she was only eight years old. Some of her verse was published in *The Gentleman's Magazine* of the day. Another sister was born with physical challenges that Charles himself never experienced, and his heart went out to her. A number of his sisters had unfortunate marriages, and in reading Charles's correspondence and poetry, one senses his deep concern for them. We know also from his *Journal* how he held them in affection and often visited them, attempting to be a companion and aid in their needs.

It may have been the way of the times that Charles and his brothers, Samuel and John, went away to school, the former two to Westminster School, and John to Charterhouse School, while the sisters were educated at home. Of course, the sisters had a gifted mentor in mother Susanna, even if one might not find all of her methods of teaching and discipline compatible with contemporary ones. What is evident in Charles's writings is his mutual respect for his sisters. They are his equals before God and the world. Granted, that was not the general view of women in eighteenth-century England, but it is not unusual to find ideas and opinions of the Wesleys that are not characteristic of the period.

Charles did not marry until he was almost forty-two years of age and, unlike his brother John's marriage, his was a mutually strengthening, enriching, and loving relationship. Charles married Sarah Gwynne on April 9, 1749, and John officiated at the wedding. Sally, as Charles called her, was indeed his intellectual and spiritual equal, a woman whose depth was empowering and challenging. Their correspondence reveals two people deeply in love, committed to one another and to God, and who truly shared their lives within the home with their children and outside it. His love poems to Sally, many of which are preserved in a manuscript titled "Courtship," are an invaluable pastoral and personal resource to those who wish to sustain a lifelong love relationship with God at the center.

Sally and Charles had eight children, only three of whom survived the dangers of infancy and childhood. Five died within the first year of life. The three surviving children were Charles Jr., Sarah (also called Sally), and Samuel. The boys revealed special musical gifts very early in life, and at a young age Sally demonstrated a penchant for poetry. There exist a number of poems by Sally that reveal why her father regularly encouraged her study and writing of poetry. It was perhaps easier for Charles to deal with his daughter's artistic gifts, which were more like his own, than those of his sons, for in his desire to provide the best of England's music education for them and to give them opportunities to perform their own compositions, he knew he would arouse the ire of many, who saw the pursuit of music as a worldly endeavor.

From daughter Sally's own letters and remarks in manuscripts, one senses the deep affection and esteem she had for her father. She was also responsible for the preservation of some of his manuscript material. Her affection ran so deep that when she discovered a poem of her father's in which he all but disowned his son Samuel for his so-called defection to Roman Catholicism, she blotted out the stanzas with ink that made this explicit. Whether this was before or after the reconciliation of father and son is not known. But she clearly wanted to remove any obstructions to healing the breach between her father and Samuel and to prevent others from knowing her father's extreme position. Of course, Charles did not write the poem for public consumption, for the writing of poetry was his own way of working through ideas, problems, concerns, conflicts, biblical interpretation, and theology in general.

In addition, it should be pointed out that numerous entries in his *MS Journal* indicate an extremely positive relationship with women who are his coequals in mission and in the Methodist societies. On page after page are entries that indicate that women were a mainstay of the early societies and that much of the work depended on them. Furthermore, Charles wrote numerous poems about women, often occasioned by death, which lifted up individual women as models for the community of the faithful.

The women in the poetry of Charles Wesley fall into two categories: women of the Bible, and women of the eighteenth century whom he remembers in tributes at the time of their death. The intent of this volume is not to present a historical survey of these women or their historical place in the early Methodist movement; rather the primary goal is to discover a literature that helps us to see the values that women had in the early Methodist movement and how those values were acknowledged, recorded, and fostered or encouraged by Charles Wesley. Where possible, their identity, family origins, and relationship to the Wesleys are noted. The title *May She Have a Word with You?* suggests that we need to hear today of their exemplary words, deeds, and lives as a whole.

These poems are not historical narratives. They are poetical responses, often written (in the case of the eighteenth-century women) on the occasion of someone's death. They are historical in the sense that we see who they were and how they practiced their Christian faith through the eyes of Charles Wesley, who held up these women to the church and larger community as models of how to live. One of the few studies that address some of the poems that appear in this volume is the article by Paul Chilcote, "Charles Wesley and Christian Practices."[1] He explores briefly the subject of Christian practices in Wesley's poems dedicated to Grace Bowen, Lady Gertrude Hotham, Mrs. Lefevre, Mary Naylor, Anne Wigginton, Hannah Dewal, Elizabeth Blackwell, Hannah Butts, and Mary Horton. Chilcote summarizes their active faith in four categories: gracious imitation (of Christ), faith working by love, holy friendship, and generous inclusivity.

Joanna Cruickshank rightfully points out that Charles "repeatedly describes the sympathetic character of the individuals he portrays"[2] in his poems. This is compatible with an eighteenth-century "culture of sensibility,"[3] which expresses itself in sympathy, compassion, and sensing or feeling the needs of others. Expressions of a "culture of sensibility" are quite obvious in the poems cited in the following chapters.

There are many similar poems written by Wesley about men who are also examples of how to live the Christian life.[4] Why not write about them here also? No doubt there is an appropriate time to do so. But eighteenth-century England was a male-dominated society, and the Church of England was a male-dominated institution. In the women of whom Charles Wesley writes in these poems we do not have simply a few extraordinary exceptions of outstanding eighteenth-century women. Yes, there is an example of the aristocracy in Lady [Caroline?] Hotham, but she is outnumbered by women who hold no place in an elite class of society. Some of them we might never have heard of were it not for Wesley's poetry about them and an occasional mention in his *MS Journal*. Therefore, it is vital to see and hear what a man of Charles's intellect and passion for Christian living has to say about these women. Even in male-dominated eighteenth-century

---

1. *PCWS* 12, 35–47.

2. Cruickshank, "'Suffering Members Sympathise,'" 248.

3. Cruickshank, "'Suffering Members Sympathise,'" 255.

4. See Cruickshank's comments on Charles's poem dedicated to Thomas Lewis (Cruickshank, "'Suffering Members Sympathise,'" 250).

England, he shows us that they are some of the noblest examples of how to live the Christian life, both then and now.

Charles had many wholesome and strong relationships with women whom he regarded with mutual respect, and it is important for the contemporary church to discover a literature that helps it to see the values women had in the early Methodist movement and how those values were acknowledged and fostered by Charles Wesley. It is the purpose of this book to ask—*May She Have a Word with You?* That is, may the women of whom Charles wrote speak once again to us in their exemplary words and lives, which Charles has preserved through his gift of poetry?

If we listen to what their lives and Christian practice have to say to us, perhaps we shall discover that they were not only women *with* a mission, but women *in* mission, for they were personifications of Christ's healing, redemptive love and service. Perhaps by listening we will want, as did Charles Wesley, to live lives like theirs.

From the eighteenth century, there is an interesting but limited bibliography of various aspects of the lives of women in the Wesleyan movement. See the selected bibliography at the conclusion of this volume.

Section 1

Women of the Bible

CHAPTER 1

Martha and Mary Magdalene

Four Poems Based on Four Lucan Passages
Luke 24:10, 10:38–39, 10:42, and 10:40

We turn first to a few poems that until 1988[1] had remained unpublished. They provide insight into Charles's interpretations of women of the Bible, which are timely and unique.

Wesley's description of Mary Magdalene and the other women who are the first to encounter the resurrected Christ is penetrating and revealing. He understands them to be more courageous than the men. They are present, and the men are not. Peter had said that he would not flee even if others did, but he was nowhere to be found. The women, however, are the first recipients of resurrected grace. They are as well the first proclaimers of the gospel news—the resurrection faith—and the first to know its power. They are furthermore the first teachers of the apostles as regards the reality of the resurrection. It is fascinating that precisely the roles that often historically have been attributed to men in the church, Wesley attributes them here to the women of Easter morning: the embodiment of courage, proclamation, and teaching (of the apostles), the latter two being the offices of *kerygma* and *didache*.

Luke 24:10: "It was Mary Magdalene—and other women which told these things unto the Apostles."

1. *UP,* 3 vols.

More courageous than the men,
 When Christ his breath resigned,
Women first the grace obtain
 Their living Lord to find;
Women first the news proclaim,
 Know his resurrection's power,
Teach th' Apostles of the Lamb
 Who lives to die no more.[2]

Martha and Mary

In the following poem, Wesley affirms Martha's faith as expressed in activity and that of Mary as expressed in contemplation. Both are blessed! Reading and musing on the word, the gathering of power in silence, are held in high esteem.

Wesley does not juxtapose these two dimensions of faith response; rather activity and contemplation are presented as complementary of one another. Indeed, "*joined* they both are blessed." In the second stanza, however, Wesley dwells more on the contemplative response, indicating that when one is able to be "excused from earthly care," this leads to the "calm repose of prayer." In addition, one studies the Scriptures and in so doing gathers all of one's powers. Therefore, such musing on the word of God is not merely a mental exercise; it is an empowering experience. Contemplation is not simply passive; it engages all of one's powers. This transpires in silence as one communes with God.

In stanza 3, as he often does, Wesley paints a picture of himself against the background of the words in stanzas 1 and 2. Here, for a moment, he imagines what it would be like to sit at Jesus' feet with his beloved ones, such as Martha and Mary. There in their midst, his entire soul is sensitized. As he listens to the Savior, he says, "All my soul is ear!"

---

2. Wesley, *MS Luke*, 350; *UP*, 2:207.

Luke 10:38–39 reads, "Martha received Him into her house. And she had a sister called Mary, who also sat at Jesus' feet, and heard his word."

Charles seems engaged in what one might call a balancing of action and contemplation, the "Martha-Mary" formula, which appears in a number of his poems about eighteenth-century women, and to which Charles sometimes adds another biblical figure, Lydia.

1. Martha's faith in active life
        Was laudably employed,
     Tending Christ with zealous strife,
        She served th' eternal God.
     Mary waiting at his feet
        The life contemplative expressed:
     Let the happy sisters meet,
        For joined they both are blessed.

2. One who Mary's lot enjoys
        Excused from earthly care
     Hearkens to his Savior's voice
        In calm repose of prayer,
     Reading, musing on the word,
        In silence gathering all his powers,
     Holds communion with his Lord,
        And God in truth adores.

3. O that I might humbly sit
        With his beloved ones,
     Happier at my Savior's feet
        Than monarchs on their thrones!
     Who before his footstool bow
        Are sure his quickening voice to hear;
     Jesus, speak: I listen now,
        And all my soul is ear![3]

3. Wesley, *MS Luke*, 159–60; *UP*, 2:123–24.

There is an additional poem by Charles written in response to Luke 10:42, which says, "But one thing is needful: and Mary hath chosen that good part, which shall not be taken away from her." Though Charles appears, as in the previous poem, to seek the balance between the activity of Martha and the contemplation of Mary, in the following poem he seems to express a preference for Mary's part. It is as though Charles understands that listening to the Redeemer's voice and adoring God through one's complete loss in love are the preface and companion to Christian activity. He avers that "Martha's chosen work is good, / But Mary's better still" (1:1–2).

In stanza 2, Wesley stresses that Mary is possessed of the "one thing needful," and speaks of this as "Mary's better part." What is the "better part?" It is to sit at the Savior's feet, the place from which no sinner can be removed. Stanza 3 stresses that this is a lifelong vocation, namely a sustained intimate fellowship with God through Jesus Christ. How is this done? It is done through praise, humble prayer, and sacrifice. Such a posture is not in contrast to Martha's part; rather it is the preface and companion to faith in action. Through this posture one sees in others the image of Christ, and as one ministers to others, one ministers to Christ. Wesley expresses this beautifully in speaking of Elizabeth Blackwell's character.

> Nursing the poor with constant care,
> Affection soft, and heart-esteem,
> She saw her Savior's image there,
> And gladly ministered to him.[4]

The intimate relationship with Christ, the ongoing fellowship evoked by listening at the Master's feet like Mary does, initiates the vision of Christ's image in others and thus motivates one to do Martha's work in service to others.

---

4. *MS FH*, 53, Part II, 7:5–8. See also *PW*, 6:327.

1.
Martha's chosen work is good,
But Mary's better still;
Mary rests on earth employed
Like those on Zion's hill,
Antedates th' immortal joys,
Partaker with the heavenly powers.
Hears her with the heavenly powers,
And lost in love adores.

2.
Rest, thou favored spirit, rest,
Who in his presence art,
Of the needful thing possessed,
And Mary's better part:
Choose who will that happy place,
He there shall unmolested sit;
Never can the Savior chase
A sinner from his feet.

3.
Here we would thro' life remain
From all distractions free,
Closest fellowship maintain
By faith and love with thee,
In the Spirit of humble prayer,
Of praise and sacrifice abide,
Till thou waft us thro' the air,
And seat us at thy side.[5]

Martha and Mary

It is indeed fascinating to read of an eighteenth-century Anglican priest speaking of a house that Christ has made a church (1:2). He seems to mean that where those of the household of faith dwell, *there is the church*, for Christ is in the midst of those present. The

5. Wesley, *MS Luke*, 103; *UP*, 2:126. Stanzas 1 and 2 appear in *PW*, 11:198.

analogy he then draws is considerably contrary to traditional views of what it means "to be church." Wesley says that those of the household of faith, the church, divide their time between secular and sacred activity, and both arenas of activity are sanctified by sacrifice and prayer.

To be sure, historically there has been, and there is still today, a debate over what constitutes secular and sacred activity, and what can truly be sanctified by sacrifice and prayer. For Wesley, there is no question, however: "*All* their works are sanctified / By sacrifice and prayer" (1:7–8). Whatever the secular tasks of Martha and Mary, they too are blessed. Nothing they do is beyond the bounds of God's blessing. Wesley clearly understood the secular and sacred activities of these two women to be within the realm of God's sanctifying grace. Does this not apply to all Christians?

> Luke 10:40: "But Martha was cumbered about much serving, and came to him," etc.

1. Blest the house, and doubly blest
        Which Christ a church hath made:
    Martha there with toils opprest
        Calls Mary to her aid:
    Wisely they their time divide
        'Twixt *secular* and *sacred* care,
    All their works are sanctified
        By sacrifice and prayer.

2. Mary could not envy feel,
        Or covet Martha's place,
    Choose the height of tumult's wheel
        Before the depth of grace:
    O might I but hear thy word
        In silence and tranquility,
    Never would I leave my Lord,
        Or turn my heart from Thee.[6]

6. Wesley, *MS Luke*, 160–61; *UP,* 2:332.

CHAPTER 2

Tabitha/Dorcas (Acts 9:36)

There follow two more poems based on a woman who appears in Acts 9:36. They concern Tabitha, or Dorcas,[1] a widow who lived in Joppa and who was known for her good works and acts of charity. The story in Acts 9 tells of her illness, death, and restoration to life. At her death, her charitable works are affirmed by the widows who come to pay tribute to her. As they stand weeping, they show the disciple Peter the garments that Tabitha had made and perhaps had given to them. Wesley understands that these are

> Works in the Spirit of Jesus done,
> In faith and love to Christ alone. (1:3–4)

Those who dedicate their lives to such "works of genuine righteousness" (2:2) condemn a world of idle dreams and emptiness by their deeds. No words are necessary.

Once again, Wesley lifts up this woman as an example of how to live. He adjures others to live as she lived, to do as she did. Those who are also full of good works, done "in faith and love to Christ alone" (1:4), like Tabitha, lay up treasures beyond this world.

Given the evil and torments of eighteenth-century England, be it the exploitation of children in the workplace, the prostitution rampant in workhouses, or the threat of robbery by highwaymen, and the injustices of a legal system fraught with corruption, it is

---

1. Tabitha is her name in Aramaic, and Dorcas is the Greek equivalent and means "gazelle."

not surprising that Wesley pleads for works of genuine righteousness. He knows that acts of good will and genuine righteousness are the most vital condemnation of life lived as "an idle dream," or "a useless tale, an empty void" (2:4–5). Therefore, if you wish to know how to live, live as did this woman.

> Acts 9:36: "This woman was full of good works, and alms-deeds which she did."

> 1. A widow on the poor bestowed
> Full of good works, divinely good,
> (Works in the Spirit of Jesus done,
> In faith and love to Christ alone)
> Who not on them, but Christ, relies,
> She lays up treasure in the skies.

> 2. Who thus to God devotes her days
> In works of genuine righteousness,
> How shall her life the world condemn
> Whose life is but an idle dream,
> A useless tale, an empty void,
> Or all for hell, not heaven, employed![2]

It is interesting that in the following poem, which is also based on the story of Tabitha in Acts 9, Wesley focuses first on the outpouring of God's power to restore life to the poor. How many widows must he have known in eighteenth-century England who lived on the edge of existence with little of life's physical resources? He is confident that God hears the cry of the poor and that the sublime divine will is to give restored life to those who least expect it. Hence, Wesley speaks of God with one of the most endearing terms in his vocabulary—"a friend to the poor" (1:8). The widow of Joppa had emulated such friendship during her life. Hence, he calls her a "woman of grace" (2:1).

---

2. Wesley, *MS Acts*, 181–82; *UP*, 2:332.

Secondly, her restored life has more than the singular purpose of personal rejuvenation. It has social implications. Others are changed; others are restored.

There is a powerful message for every age in this little poem, for it affirms that restoring life to the poor is one of the Christian's most desired and valued vocations, and deeds of charity to the poor endure and have the power to transform. For every life restored, especially among the poor, many more lives will be changed.

Acts 9:41–42: "He presented her alive. And it was known throughout all Joppa; and many believed in the Lord."

1. God hearkens, and hears
    The sorrowful saints
Replies to their tears,
    And troubles, and wants;
God's only good pleasure
    Doth freely restore
An heavenly treasure
    A friend to the poor.

2. One woman of grace
    To life is restored
That many may praise
    And turn to the Lord;
A single believer
    From death they receive,
That thousands forever
    With Jesus may live.[3]

3. Wesley, *MS Acts*, 184; *UP,* 2:333.

CHAPTER 3

The Woman of Canaan (Matthew 15)

Among the women of the Bible to whom Charles Wesley pays a lyrical tribute is the Canaanite woman of Matthew 15. This is Charles's poetical interpretation of Jesus and a woman thought to be outside the fold of Israel. Here one finds the confrontation of two worlds: Jews and gentiles. Every stanza of the poem is written in the first person, as if the woman were speaking in each one to Jesus, to whom she refers with the messianic term, "Son of David." Only in the last two stanzas does Jesus speak to her, emphasizing the silence of Jesus in the biblical account of Matthew, "Still thou answerest not a word / To my repeated prayer" (2:1–2).

She is fully aware of her social and ethnic context and identity. A "Canaanite by birth," she desired to be saved from the tyranny of social division. The prayer that Wesley places in her mouth at the end of the first four stanzas is:

> Mercy, mercy upon me
> Thou Son of David have. (1:7–8)

Though she is not of the house of Israel, forcefully she says to Jesus, "Still I follow thee, and pray . . . Ever crying after thee" (3:3, 5).

Wesley is very clear about the strong message she personifies in the Gospel of Matthew. God's covenant is not limited to Israel's fold alone. She says to Jesus,

> To the sheep of Israel's fold
>> Thou in thy flesh wast sent,
>> In thee their covenant. (4:1–3)

Therefore, she says, "See me then, with pity see, / A sinner, whom thou cam'st to save" (4:4–5).

There is an interesting theological shift in stanzas 5 through 9, namely to the Wesleyan emphasis of "free grace." This is most certainly Charles's imprint of Wesleyan and Arminian language on the story. In stanzas 5 through 7, the concluding words of the Canaanite woman's pleas to Jesus are, "Thy grace is free for all" (5:8, 6:8, 7:8).

The troubling passage for interpreters, namely Jesus' reference to casting children's bread to dogs, is addressed somewhat differently by Wesley. The implication is, of course, that gentiles are seen as dogs, and they may eat the crumbs that fall from their Master's table. In stanza 8, however, Charles has the Canaanite woman bid Jesus:

> Give me living bread to eat,
>> And say, in answer to my call,
>> "Canaanite, thy faith is great,
>>> My grace is free for all." (8:5–8)

What is fascinating about Wesley's structure of the last two stanzas (8 and 9) is that Jesus' words "great is your faith" are placed in the mouth of the Canaanite woman. It is as if she says to Jesus, this is what you should say to me:

> "Canaanite, thy faith is great,
>> My grace is free for all." (8:7–8)

Stanza 9 begins with the conditional phrase, "If thy grace for all is free," let me hear your call. Then she says,

> Now the gracious word repeat,
>> The word of healing to my soul,
>> "Canaanite, thy faith is great,
>>> Thy faith hath made thee whole." (9:5–8)

What is so interesting about the structure of this poem is that we hear Jesus' words uttered by someone outside the fold of Israel, and not in a derogatory manner. The image here is that this is what gentiles hear Jesus saying to them. Namely, they are included because grace is free for all.

The Woman of Canaan[1]
[Matthew 15:22, &c.]

1.   Lord, regard my earnest cry,
           A potsherd of the earth,
       A poor guilty worm am I,
           A Canaanite by birth:
       Save me from this tyranny,
   From all the power of Satan save,
       Mercy, mercy upon me
           Thou Son of David have.

2.   Still thou answerest not a word
           To my repeated prayer;
       Hear thy own disciples, Lord,
           Who in my sorrows share,
       O let them prevail with thee
   To grant the blessing which I crave:
       Mercy, mercy [upon me
           Thou Son of David have.]

3.   Send, O send me now away,
           By granting my request,
       Still I follow thee, and pray,
           And will not let thee rest,
       Ever crying after thee,
   Till thou my helplessness relieve,
       Mercy, mercy [upon me
           Thou Son of David have.]

1. *HSP* 1742, 96–98.

4.   To the sheep of Israel's fold
           Thou in thy flesh wast sent,
        In thee their covenant.
     See me then, with pity see,
   A sinner, whom thou cam'st to save;
        Mercy, mercy [upon me
           Thou Son of David have.]

5.   Still to thee, my God, I come,
           And mercy I implore,
        Thee (but how shall I presume)
           Thee trembling I adore,
        Dare not stand before thy face,
     But lowly at thy feet I fall,
        Help me, Jesu, shew thy grace!
           Thy grace is free for all.

6.   Still I cannot part with thee,
           I will not let thee go,
        Mercy, mercy unto me,
           O Son of David shew,
        Vilest of the sinful race,
     On thee importunate I call,
        Help me, Jesu, shew thy grace,
           Thy grace is free for all.

7.   Nothing am I in thy sight,
           Nothing have I to plead,
        Unto dogs it is not right
           To cast the children's bread:
        Yet the dogs the crumbs may eat,
     That from their master's table fall,
        Let the fragments be my meat,
           Thy grace is free for all.

8.   Give me, Lord, the victory,
My heart's desire fulfill;
Let it now be done to me
According to my will,
Give me living bread to eat,
And say, in answer to my call,
"Canaanite, thy faith is great,
My grace is free for all."

9.   If thy grace for all is free,
Thy call now let me hear,
Shew this token upon me,
And bring salvation near;
Now the gracious word repeat,
The word of healing to my soul,
"Canaanite, thy faith is great,
Thy faith hath made thee whole."

Section 2

Women of the Eighteenth Century

CHAPTER 4

Grace Bowen

d. January 2, 1755

Charles Wesley's poems occasioned by the deaths of women are indeed a treasury of spirituality, for they hold up these women as models of faith to the gospel community, that it may know how to live out the mandate of Christian love and service. They are exemplary of the inclusive nature of ministry and mission. They relate how life should be lived and how time should be spent.

Grace Bowen (d. 1755) of Garth and Ludlow was the nurse of Mrs. Charles Wesley and is mentioned by Charles a number of times in his journal and letters to his wife. He mentions her as a friend, as one of the faithful, whose endurance of suffering is exemplary.[1]

In the poem "On the Death of Mrs. Grace Bowen," Wesley emphasizes that it is the legacy we leave behind in this world that matters, and this woman leaves a rich one. He is so moved by it that he wants to live and die as she did. At the outset of her pilgrimage "She lived to serve the God unknown" and thought that she could *buy* the peace of God through good works. However, the decisive realization in her life was that God had done for her what she could not do for herself, namely he simply had given her fulfilling peace through Jesus Christ, and this peace was a gift, nothing she

1. See the *MS Journal*, 2:260, 270.

could earn. From the moment of that realization began "the fight of faith" (6:1). Yet, no matter what storm raged, she withstood it.

The faith of Mrs. Bowen was an "active faith"[2] (8:2) revealed in one who loved in word and deed. So thoroughly was she imbued with God's love that whatever she had was seen as a "treasure for the poor" (10:3).

What is so memorable about her legacy? Warmth, eagerness to guide others into right paths, kind counsel, warning fears, loud protests, silent tears, and love of God alone. Another aspect of her legacy that deeply moved Wesley is that he recognized that her only real fear was that amid suffering she might complain. He longs for the triumph of her death for himself and all Christians. As painful as death may be for loved ones remaining on earth, death means union with God the Creator. What greater joy can there be! Certainly, one despairs and longs for "A mother of our Israel gone" (Part II, 8:7), but she still speaks to us. Her unwavering faith, genuine love, and meek humility remind us that we should live her life and die her death.

Furthermore, we should see Grace Bowen as our guardian angel.

> She took your guardian angel's part,
> She watched the motions of your heart,
>   To pride and pleasure prone;
> For you she spent her latest breath,
> And urged you both in life and death
>   To love the Lord alone. (Part I, 14:1–6)

Wesley would have us dwell on her image, "on which even angels gaze" (Part II, 1:3), that we may be presented to God as faithful and mature saints.

---

2. See Chilcote's section on "Active Faith." Chilcote, "Charles Wesley and Christian Practices," 44.

On the Death of Mrs. Grace Bowen[3]
January 2d, 1755

Part I

1. Stay, thou triumphant spirit, stay
   And bless me e'er thou soar'st away,
     Where pain can never come.
   In vain my call; the soul is fled,
   By Israel's flaming steeds conveyed
     To her eternal home.

2. Yet lo, I now the blessing find,
   The legacy she left behind,
     Fruit of her latest prayer:
   The answer in my heart I feel,
   This fresh supply of heavenly zeal,
     To live and die like her.

3. She lived to serve the God unknown,
   And following in a land not sown,
     A thorny wilderness,
   Beneath the yoke of legal fear
   She labored hard, with heart sincere,
     To *buy*[4] the Savior's peace.

4. Faithful she then in little was,
   And zealous for religion's cause,
     To please the Lord most high
   In serving all she humbly sought,
   But blindly by her duties thought
     Herself to justify.

---

3. *FH* 1759, 23–28. *MS Journal,* 2:560, 570.

4. Unless otherwise noted, all italics that appear in Wesley's works in this book are his own.

5. Yet when she heard the Gospel-sound,
    That grace doth more than sin abound,
      That pardoning grace is free,
    She cast her righteous rags aside,
    She closed at once with Christ, and cried,
      "He bought the peace for me!"

6. From hence the fight of faith began,
    From hence in Jesus' steps she ran,
      Nor e'er disgraced the cause;
    Meek follower of the patient Lamb,
    She prized his honorable shame,
      And gloried in his cross.

7. By all the rage of fiends and men,
    (The vehement stream, the beating rain,)
      Assailed on every side;
    Nor men or fiends her firmness shock,
    The house was built upon a rock,
      And every storm defied.

8. What tongue her hidden worth can tell,
    Her active faith, and fervent zeal,
      And works of righteousness;
    Her thirst and reverence for the word,
    Her love to those who loved her Lord,
      Or but desired his grace?

9. She loved them in both word and deed,
    O'erjoyed an hungry Christ to feed,
      To visit Him in pain;
    Him in his members she relieved,
    And freely as she first received,
      Gave him her all again.

10. How did her generous bounty deal
     The widow's scanty oil and meal,
       A treasure for the poor!
     A treasure, spent without decrease,
     As miracle revived to bless
       The consecrated store.

11. But who can paint the strong desire,
     The holy heaven-enkindled fire
       That glowed within her breast,
     T' insure the bliss of friends and foes,
     To save the precious souls of those
       She ever loved the best?

12. Witness, ye children of her prayers,
     Ye objects of her tenderest cares,
       Into her bosom given;
     Did not her yearning bowels move,
     With more than a material love,
       To train you up for heaven?

13. Can you her artless warmth forget,
     Her eager haste to turn your feet
       Into the narrow road;
     Her counsels kind, her warning fears,
     Her loud protests, or silent tears,
       Whene'er ye strayed from God?

14. She took your guardian angel's part,
     She watched the motions of your heart,
       To pride and pleasure prone;
     For you she spent her latest breath,
     And urged you both in life and death
       To love the Lord alone.

Part II

1.   O let me on the image dwell,
     The soul-transporting spectacle
       On which even angels gaze!
    A faithful saint mature for God,
    And shaking off the earthly clod,
      To see God's open face.

2.   The happiest hour is come at last,
    When, all her toils and conflicts past,
      She shall to God ascend;
    Worn out and spent for Jesus' cause,
    She now takes up her latest cross,
      And bears it to the end.

3.   Summoned before the throne to appear,
    She meets the welcome messenger,
      Arrayed in mortal pain;
    Her only fear lest flesh and blood
    Should sink beneath the sacred load,
      Or weakly once complain.

4.   But Christ, the object of her love,
    Doth with peculiar smiles approve,
      And all her fears control;
    With glory gilds her final scene,
    And not a cloud can rise between,
      To hide him from her soul.

5.   As a ripe shock of corn brought home,
    Behold her in due season come
      To claim her full reward!
    Smiling and pleased in death she lies,
    With eagle's eyes looks through the skies,
      And sees her heavenly Lord.

6. The sight her ravished spirit fires,
    Her panting, dying breast inspires,
        And fills her mouth with praise;
    She owns the glorious earnest given,
    The hidden life breaks out, and heaven
        Resplendent in her face.

7. Filled up with love and life divine,
    The house of clay, the earthly shrine,
        Dissolves, and sinks to dust;
    Without a groan the body dies,
    Her spirit mounts above the skies,
        And mingles with the just.

8. With mixed concern her flight we view,
    With joy the ascending pomp pursue,
        Yet for *our* loss distressed:
    Our bosom friend from earth is flown,
    A mother of our Israel gone
        To her eternal rest.

9. Yet still to us she speaks, though dead;
    She bids us in her footsteps tread,
        As in her Savior's she;
    And, O that we like her may prove
    Our faith unfeigned, and genuine love,
        And meek humility.

10. Who live her life, her death shall die;
    Come, Lord, our hearts to certify
        That we the prize shall gain;
    Soon as we lay the body down,
    That we shall wear the immortal crown,
        And in thy glory reign.

CHAPTER 5

Lady [Caroline?] Hotham[1]

d. June 30, 1756

Lady Gertrude Hotham of London was the wife of Sir Charles Hotham, who once promised Charles Wesley Jr., the gift of an organ; however, not long afterward he went abroad and died. Charles Wesley laments, "With him Charles [his son] lost all hope and prospect of a benefactor."[2] She was an admirer of Charles Jr. and "made him a present of all her music."[3]

What is it about the life of Lady [Caroline?] Hotham that bids Charles place her life before us to be remembered in verse? *She is a woman of "patient faith"* (Part I, 5:3; italics mine), which leads to union with God. Wesley feels deeply the loss of this faithful servant and declares: "We only fear to *lose our loss*" (Part I, 8:1; italics his). What does he mean? That the pain of the loss of this woman of patient faith would one day vanish. That would be a tragic loss of memory—that her exemplary life would no longer be recalled.

She is a woman of virtue, a faithful saint of whom Charles Wesley does not want to lose sight. Lady Hotham is a woman whose soul is endowed with meek, obedient awe toward God.

---

1. Lady Gertrude Hotham (1696–1775) was the widow of Sir Charles Hotham (1693–1738), the Fifth Baronet of Scarborough and daughter of Phillip Stanhope, the third Earl of Chesterfield. Lady Hotham was a Methodist sympathizer and became known for her prayer meetings held at Campdet House. She became a friend of the Charles Wesley family and included him in her will. It is assumed that the poem was dedicated to her daughter, Caroline, perhaps, in part, to comfort the mother.

2. *MS Journal,* 2:142.

3. *MS Journal,* 2:142.

Would that it could be said of every human being what Wesley says of her,

> Her from the birth the Lord did draw;
> God's Spirit meek, obedient awe
> Her tender soul endowed;
> God fixed the principle within,
> The love of truth, the dread of sin,
> The hunger after God. (Part II, 2:1–6)

She was *"entirely ruled by grace"* (Part II, 4:1; italics mine) and sought neither notoriety nor recognition. She was "a secret saint, unknown" (Part II, 4:3), a stranger to pride and selfishness, and she had a singular purpose—to live for God alone. Whoever came into contact with her encountered the peace of a dove, and she was so filled with the love of God that she was unaware that her every word and action were formed by it. Hence, she was "Hid from herself by grace divine" (Part II, 6:4).

Her memorial is the portrait of her "engraven in our heart" (Part III, 1:6): *she denied herself to serve others.* It was her "sacred, social character" (Part III, 4:2) that displayed the mystery of Jesus whom "she loved, revered, obeyed" (Part III, 4:6). Having so lived, she confidently anticipated life forever with God. Social character and eternal life are intimately related!

Once again, Wesley remembers a model life for the community of faith by pointing to its social character. Lady Hotham was "so wholly formed for social love" (Part V, 4:1) that the poet wonders what angel could even praise her union with God. Those who are so formed experience oneness with God forever! Like her they become "with God forever one" (Part V, 8:6)! It is not surprising that Wesley should conclude his poetical praise of her life with the dimension of "social love," for an insular, isolated love cannot be God's love expressed in Jesus Christ. His love is "social love" that goes in search of all human beings at all costs, even death upon a cross.

Wesley understands that Lady Hotham's life gives us hope. It is the resurrected life personified; hence, it must be remembered.

On the Death of Lady Hotham[4]
June 30th, 1756

Part I

1. Father, thy righteous will be done!
   To make thy righteous will our own,
      We patiently resign
   The object of our softest care,
   The daughter of our faith and prayer,
      The dearest gift divine.

2. Unworthy of the blessing lent,
   Her, from our bleeding bosom rent,
      For ours no more we claim;
   Whom mortals could not duly prize,
   Joined to her kindred in the skies,
      And married to the Lamb.

3. Here lovely excellence is fled,
   And leaves the dead t' intomb the dead
      T' embalm them with our tears.
   An lo, with softly pensive pace
   We measure out our mournful days
      Till Israel's Car appears.

4. The Car that carried up our Friend,
   The flaming host shall soon descend
      Our spirits to remove,
   Then we again our Friend shall find,
   In love indissolubly joined
      To her who reigns above.

---

4. The poem was published posthumously in *PW*, 6:292–300; see *MS FH*, 1–9. See Wesley's brief poem dedicated to Lady Gertrude Hotham in *AM* 2 (1779): 545.

5. Through God who called her up to reign,
   We too th' immortal crown shall gain,
       On patient faith bestowed;
   We trust the Lamb shall bring us through,
   And hasten to the blissful view
       Of a redeeming God.

6. Till then, disdaining all relief,
   And brooding on our sacred grief,
       We quietly endure
   The pangs of loss, the lingering smart,
   The anguish of a broken heart,
       Which only heaven can cure.

7. Help us, thou heavenly Man of woe,
   Unwearied in thy steps to go,
       To mix our tears with thine,
   To drink thine agonizing cup,
   To fill thine after-sufferings up
       And die the death Divine.

8. We only fear to *lose our loss*;
   The burden of our heaviest cross
       Through life we fain would bear;
   Would feel the ever-recent wound,
   And weeping at thy feet be found,
       And die lamenting there.

Part II

1. Still let us on her virtue gaze,
   With sad delight and wonder trace

The favorite of the skies,
The child that lives her hundred years,
A faithful saint to God appears,
And filled with glory dies.

2. Her from the birth the Lord did draw;
God's Spirit with meek, obedient awe
Her tender soul endowed;
God fixed the principle within,
The love of truth, the dread of sin,
The hunger after God.

3. While nature's will remained alive,
God never ceased to check and strive,
And heavenly power impart;
Her heart from evil God withheld,
Till love divine the world expelled
Forever from her heart.

4. Thenceforth, entirely ruled by grace,
She swiftly ran her heavenly race,
A secret saint unknown;
Stranger to pride and selfish art,
In singleness of eye and heart
She lived to God alone.

5. Whoe'er beheld, pronounced her blest;
Her walk on earth the Lamb confessed,
The wisely simple dove,
The soul composed in Jesus' peace,
That only languished to possess
The fullness of God's love.

6. Unconscious of the love bestowed,
   Whence all her words and actions flowed,
      She made her humble moan;
   Hid from herself by grace divine,
   How sweetly did she wail and pine
      To find the God unknown!

7. Known by her God, and well approved
   God's[5] servants for God's sake she loved,
      God's messengers received;
   From death to life her passage showed,
   By owning all who owned her God,
      And in God's Spirit lived.

8. For them she toiled with Martha's hands,
   Yet list'ning for her Lord's commands
      of Mary's part possessed,
   Till Jesus called her at his feet,
   Spake her glad soul for glory meet,
      and caught her to his breast.

Part III

1. Go, blessed saint, to Jesus go,
   Transported from the vale below,
      Thou canst not quite depart;
   Thy fair memorial stays behind,
   Thy lovely portraiture we find
      Engraven on our heart.

2. The friend by grace and nature dear,
   The cordial friend, doth still appear,

---

5. "God's" in lines 2 and 3 = "his" in original.

Though ravished from our sight;
On earth a guardian angel found,
Diffusing bliss to all around,
     And ministering delight.

3. As born her relatives to please,
    Her own delight, and choice, and ease,
         She cheerfully denied;
    Servant of all, rejoiced to stoop,
    Filled each domestic duty up,
         And every part supplied.

4. But shining in her properest sphere,
    (The sacred, social character,)
         The mystery she displayed
    Of Jesus by the church adored,
    While next to Christ her earthly Lord,
         She loved, revered, obeyed.

5. She more than shared his woe and weal,
    Attentive to his safety still,
         Engrossed by *his alone,*
    Her time, her thoughts, her health she gave,
    Till, his far dearer life to save,
         She sacrificed her own.

6. 'Twas aimed at him the deadly dart,
    But glancing missed his fearless heart
         and pierced her faithful side;
    Eager her Consort to redeem,
    She sickened, and declined for him,
         for him she drooped and died.

7. Conscious of dissolution near,
    Above all pain, regret, and fear,
        Her paradise restored
    She found with Jesus in her heart,
    And calmly languished to depart,
        And see her heavenly Lord.

8. "Ready to fly this moment home,
    If Thou, my Savior, bidd'st me come,
        Me if Thou wilt receive,
    Poorest of all thy creatures me;
    And surely now thou say'st, with Thee
        I shall forever live."

9. She spoke, and by her looks expressed
    The glorious everlasting rest
        To saints triumphant given;
    Glided in ecstasies away,
    And told us, through her smiling clay,
        My soul is fled to heaven!

Part IV

1. Then let us look with comfort up,
    Not sorrowing as bereft of hope,
        But bowed by God's decree:
    O God, thy love, severely kind,
    Calls off our hearts from earth to find
        Their bliss complete in Thee.

2. From her and every creature torn,
    Blessed with the privilege to mourn,
        In calm submission kept;
    Softened, we feel the sacred woe,
    Which God himself vouchsafed to know,
        And weep as Jesus wept.

3. His tears relieve our mournful pain,
   His word, "Your friend shall rise again,"
       Puts every care to flight:
   Thou wilt, O God, fulfill his word,
   And bring her back, with Christ our Lord,
       And all the saints in light.

4. Her soul we shall embrace once more,
   (How changed from her we knew before,
       The Godhead's earthly shrine!)
   Distinguished by peculiar rays,
   The image shining on her face,
       The glorious Name Divine.

5. Met in those permanent abodes,
   Secure we live the life of gods,
       Of bliss without alloy:
   No pining want, or soft excess,
   No tender tear to damp our peace,
       Or death to kill our joy.

6. Sorrow, and sin, and death are dead,
   And sighing is forever fled,
       When life's last gasp is o'er;
   When that celestial port we gain,
   Sickness, infirmity, and pain,
       And parting is no more.

7. O that we all were landed there!
   We only wait till Christ prepare
       His dearly purchased bride.
   Come, Lord, and change and take us hence,

And give us an inheritance
  Among the sanctified.

8. We know Thou wilt not long delay
  To bear our ready souls away;
    And when we meet above,
  Our full inheritance be Thou;
  But bless us with the earnest now,
    The seal of perfect love.

Part V

1. O wondrous power of Jesus' grace,
  Who sends an angel from his face
    With ministerial aid!
  By faith in brightest glory seen,
  She pours the balm of comfort in,
    And heals the wound she made.

2. The blessed spirit enthroned above
  (Whom far beyond ourselves we love,
    Soon as her bliss appears)
  Scatters the gloom of nature's grief,
  Brings irresistible relief,
    And dries our selfish tears.

3. Her bliss no pause nor period knows,
  Her bliss our ravished heart o'erflows;
    The heavenly drop we feel
  Is more than thousand worlds can give:
  Who then shall all her joy conceive,
    Or all her raptures tell?

4. *So wholly formed for social love,*[6]
   Her union with the spirits above
      What angel can declare?
   Her joy, amidst the virgin-choir,
   To mark a saint in white attire,
      To clasp a sister there!

5. With her to range th' eternal plains;
   To catch the harpers' sweetest strains,
      And match them with her own;
   Pursue the living water's course,
   Or trace the river to its source,
      And drink it at the throne.

6. There, there the ecstasy is full,
   While, wide expanding all her soul,
      The Godhead she receives;
   Enjoys th' unutterable grace,
   Beholds without a veil God's face,
      Beholds God's face and lives.

7. For this on earth she could not rest,
   (With every other blessing blest,)
      Or in God's gifts delight;
   Not holiness itself could sate
   The spirit constrained in bliss to wait,
      Without that blissful sight.

8. But, gaining now whom she requires,
   She all her infinite desires
      Lets loose on God alone;
   She plunges in the crystal sea,
   Lost in the depths of Deity,
      With God forever one!

6. Italics added for emphasis.

CHAPTER 6

Mrs. L[efevre]

d. July 6, 1756

Wesley tells us in his memorial to Mrs. L[efevre] that she died at the young age of thirty-three, as did Jesus. Hers was a sudden death that cut short her "excellence" (Part I, 1:3). Who was she? A burning and shining light that "set our world on fire" (Part I, 4:6). She was a woman of lamblike spirit who was bestowed with love invincible, love that turns the other cheek, love that is meek and bears and conquers all things.

Wesley is so overcome with the impact of her love-perfected life that he says "words can never paint" who she was. But then he paints with the brush of his own poetical art one of the most eloquent pictures of a life to be found in the entire corpus of his verse:

> She *was* (what words can never paint)
> A spotless soul, a sinless saint,
>   In perfect love renewed;
> A mirror of the Deity,
> A transcript of the One in Three,
>   A temple filled with God. (Part I, 5:1–6)

The first line of the poem describes her as "a Christ-like soul." Who could be more like Christ than one who is "a spotless soul, a sinless saint?" Wesley holds up her life before us that we too, like her, might be renewed in perfect love, become mirrors of the Deity, transcripts of the Holy Trinity, and a temple filled with God. Here is a superb summary of the life of holiness.

How happy we would be, if we could find the secret, as did she, "to gain by every loss." Perhaps this is indeed what it means to glory in the cross of Christ. Hence, Wesley prays that the mantle of her life will be dropped on us, that our heart's desire will be "daily in her steps to tread."

We have a clue to the importance of Wesley's poems that celebrate the lives of others, when he concludes by imploring God:

> Made ready here, by patient love,
> For sweetest fellowship above
>   With our translated friend,
> Give us through life her spirit to breathe,
> Indulge us then to die her death,
>   And bless us with her end. (Part II, 6:1–6)

We cannot leave this memorable poem, however, without pointing to the pastoral counsel Wesley gives regarding grief. We must be ready to unleash our grief and let it pour out of our inner being. Though our tenderest nerve is pricked by anguish, we must not conceal our feelings; rather let our tears flow. Of course, here they are tears of "universal loss" (Part I, 3:3), yet tears of joy, when one recalls the life of love she lived.

On the Death of Mrs. L[efevre],[1]

July 6th, 1756

Part I

1. Ah! lovely Christ-like soul, adieu,
    Darling of every heart that knew
        Thy short-lived excellence;
    Rest in the bosom of thy God,
    Who just to gazing mortals showed,
        And snatched the wonder hence.

---

1. *FH* 1759, 46–48. A manuscript copy of this hymn in Wesley's script is found in his own copy of *Letters upon Sacred Subjects*. The copy bears Wesley's signature and the date 1757.

2.   Unworthy of her longer stay,
     Forbid to plead, forbid to pray,
       We mournfully resign
     Our friend, so suddenly removed;
     We render to her Best-beloved
       The heavenly loan divine.

3.   But *need* we now our grief conceal,
     Forced in the tenderest nerve to feel
       The universal loss?
     We *cannot* curb our swelling sighs,
     Or stop the fountains of our eyes,
       Remembering what she *was.*

4.   She *was* (let all her worth confess,
     Let all her precious memory bless,
       And after her aspire!)
     A burning and a shining light—
     She *was*—to gild our land of night,
       And set our world on fire.

5.   She *was* (what words can never paint)
     A spotless soul, a sinless saint,
       In perfect love renewed;
     A mirror of the Deity,
     A transcript of the One in Three,
       A temple filled with God;

6.   The witness of his hallowing grace,
     Talked with her Maker face to face,
       And marked with his new name
     His nature visibly expressed,
     While all her even life confessed
       The meekness of the Lamb.

7. Blessed with his lowly loving mind,
   One with the friend of human kind,
     In all his steps she trod;
   In doing good, and bearing ill,
   Fulfilled her heavenly Father's will,
     And lived, and died to God.

8. Eager to drink Christ's deepest cup,
   She filled her Lord's affliction up,
     Together crucified;
   To nature's will entirely dead,
   She languished till she bowed her head,
     And with her Savior died.

9. Like Him, her *thirty years and three*
   She finished on the sacred tree,
     In sacrificial prayer;
   Calmly, without a lingering sigh,
   Dismissed her spirit to the sky,
     And clasps her Jesus there.

Part II

1. O that the child of heavenly light
   Might drop her mantle in her flight,
     Her lamb-like spirit leave!
   On us let all her graces rest,
   To meeken every troubled breast,
     And teach us how to grieve.

2. Happy, could we the secret find,
   Like her in all events resigned,

To gain by every loss;
Our sharpest agonies t' improve,
Esteem our Master's lot, and love,
And glory in, His cross.

3. Master, on us, even us, bestow
Like precious faith, thyself to know;
Fulfill our heart's desire,
Daily in all her steps to tread;
And let us in the garden bleed,
And on the mount expire.

4. Like her, who now, supremely blest,
Enjoys an everlasting rest,
We fain on earth would be;
As harmless as that gentlest dove,
As simplified by humble love,
As perfectly like thee.

5. O were it, Lord, on us bestowed,
The love that in her bosom glowed,
The love invincible;
The love that turns the other cheek,
The love inviolably meek,
That bears and conquers all!

6. Made ready here, by patient love,
For sweetest fellowship above
With our translated friend,
Give us through life her spirit to breathe,
Indulge us then to die her death,
And bless us with her end.

CHAPTER 7

Mrs. Mercy Thornton

d. March 1, 1757

Here Wesley combines an affirmation of faith with a brief description of Mercy Thornton's practice of the vocation of doing God's will, which is a model for us.

The poem opens with the affirmation from "The Lord's Prayer": "Th' Almighty will be done" (1:1). In her earnest longing after God and the exercise of the divine will, Mercy Thornton became the recipient of God's self-disclosure through the revelation of the mysterious name: "Jesus, Jah/Jehovah" (3:3), Spirit. *Jah* (*YH*, a shortened form of Hebrew *YHWH*, the unpronounceable Hebrew name for God sometimes vocalized as "Jehovah" and sometimes translated as "Lord"), Jehovah's Son Jesus, and God the Spirit, i.e., the Holy Trinity, become the breath of her life. Wesley concludes the faith affirmation of the God who is revealed to her, and whom she adored and served, with words reminiscent of the Nicene Creed:

> God of God, and Light of Light,
>> Christ the one eternal God. (4:5–6)

The revelation of this Light brings Mercy Thornton the awareness that God has a singular purpose for existence—redemption. And in the knowledge of that redemption she finds triumph in the cross of Christ and humility in walking in his footsteps.

Her sole purpose is to do God's will. The course of doing God's will is one of patient love. How does she pursue this course?

(a) With eagerness and composure, (b) with a strong will against opponents of Christ, (c) by bearing the burden of those who disown Christ, and (d) by praying for them in her last and dying prayer, which was her last work of love.

Thanks to Wesley, we can remember the affirmation of God that she lived, and we can seek to follow her example.

On the Death of Mrs. Mercy Thornton,[1]
March 1, 1757

1. The' Almighty will be done,
    Who justly claims God's own!
        Sister, daughter, friend, farewell!
    Caught up to thy great reward,
        To the bliss ineffable,
    To the bosom of thy Lord.

2. Beyond our vale of woe,
    Detached from all below,
        Long thy gracious soul aspired
    After God's beloved embrace,
        Restlessly its God required,
    Gasped to see God's glorious face.

3. No *new-made* Deity,
    He showed himself to thee,
        Jesus, Jah, Jehovah came,
    Pleased God's nature to impart,
        Told thee the mysterious name,
    Breathed God's Spirit into thy heart.

4. Through his own Spirit's power,
    Thou didst thy Lord adore,

1. *FH* 1759, 14–16.

With unborrowed glories bright,
Dwelling in an earthly clod,
   God of God, and Light of Light,
Christ the one eternal God.

5. God over all supreme,
Almighty to redeem,
   The first, self-existing cause,
God thou didst divinely know,
   Daily triumph in Christ's cross,
Humbly in his footsteps go.

6. Thy meat was to fulfill
The heavenly Father's will:
   Sent to do his will alone,
O, how swiftly didst thou move,
   Eager, yet composed, to run
All the course of patient love!

7. In meek and quiet peace,
Thou didst thy soul possess;
   Far from every wild extreme
Thy substantial piety:
   Never could the world blaspheme,
Never scoff the truth for thee.

8. Close follower of the Lamb,
Whose love the world o'ercame,
   Them thou didst, like him, oppose,
Conquering all their ill with good,
   Melting down the Savior's foes,
Foes that trampled on His blood.

9. The man who dare disown
    God's co-eternal Son,
        Meet and ready to depart,
    Didst thou not their burden bear?
        Grieved for them thy bleeding heart,
    Sighed for them thy dying prayer.

10. That latest labor o'er,
    Thy spirit strives no more;
        Finished her great work of love,
    Lo, she quits the house of clay,
        Claps her wings, and soars above,
    Mingles with eternal day!

CHAPTER 8

Mary Naylor

d. March 21, 1757

Mary Naylor is mentioned a number of times in Charles Wesley's *Journal* and his letters, especially to his wife Sally. She is a trusted friend and faithful Christian who is called upon to counsel a wayward woman, to assist in one instance with financial matters of the Charles Wesley family, and a friend and guest in the Wesley home. No doubt the length of this poem indicates the depth of Charles Wesley's Christian affection for this woman of faith.

Charles Wesley devotes fifty stanzas of six lines each (300 lines) and a shorter additional poem of six stanzas of four lines—each in a different meter—to Mary Naylor. Without question, she made a tremendous impression on him and he felt compelled to commend her life as an example of how to live and die. If we want to know how to live and die, hers is the life to "keep in view" (Part I, 2:4), says Wesley. Why? What does her life tell us we should do with our own?

(1) *Learn life's true meaning early.* At first, she had thought life was only a "time to play" (Part I, 3:4). Hence, she ignored Christ and the things of God. But once she heard God's word, it was "engrafted" (Part I, 4:3) in her heart. This enabled her to grow in "solid piety" (Part I, 8:1) and to overcome hatred with love.

(2) *Exercise faithful stewardship over gifts and resources.* She studied diligently to improve her talents, to grow in faith, love, holiness, and prayer, and she tithed.

(3) *Pursue justice and the golden rule.*

The golden rule she has pursued,
and did to others as she would
others should do to her:
justice composed her upright soul,
justice did all her thoughts control,
and formed her character. (Part II, 3:1–6)

She learned the "love of equity" (Part II, 4:4) for all and opposed falsehood, pretense, show, and lying.

(4) *Practice keen judgment and speak with candor and love.* Mary Naylor did not expend her strength for nothing, but learned to live by the highest priorities.

(5) *Show mercy and empathy to all, especially those in distress.* She was a "nursing-mother to the poor" (Part III, 4:1) who gave her own bread to "friend and foe" (Part III, 5:6). Through her own outstretched arms of charity, she grew in grace and love. Wesley says, "I want to love my foes, like her" (Part VI, 9:1). Chilcote quotes the first four stanzas of Part III as evidence of Mary Naylor's faithful Christian practice, particularly "hospitality, testimony, forgiveness, healing, social service, sick visitation, prison ministry, and generosity."[1]

(6) *Be constant in character.* According to Wesley, she was "invariably the same" (Part III, 8:3), a woman of patient faith and even mind.

(7) *Grow in insight to be able to see through "superficial grace,"* (Part IV, 5:4) as claimed and practiced by some.

(8) *Be prepared to die.* Mary Naylor knew she had already entered eternal life in this world, for it is a present possession.

"Nothing," she cries, "can shake my peace,
My body or my soul distress,
Or tempt me once to fear,
My full salvation is wrought out,
I cannot mourn, I cannot doubt,
For Christ and heaven are here." (Part V, 6:1–6)

---

1. Chilcote, "Charles Wesley and Christian Practices," 42.

What prepared her so well for death? Trust in God, not herself; meekness and the willingness to take the burdens of others and "our bleeding hearts" (Part V, 8:5) to the heart of God. Charles Wesley yearns, as should all, to die like Mary Naylor:

> O might thy censurers, and I
> Obtain the grace, like thee to die,
>   And kiss thy feet in heaven. (Part VI, 5:4–6)

On the Death of Mrs. Mary Naylor[2]
March 21st, 1757.

Part I

1. But is the hasty spirit fled?
    But hath my friend inclined her head,
        And laid her burden down?
    Dead, dead to man, to God she lives,
    And from her Savior's hands receives
        The never-fading crown.

2. Away, my tears and selfish sighs!
    The happy saint in paradise
        Requires us not to mourn;
    But rather keep her life in view,
    And still her shining steps pursue,
        Till all to God return.

3. Her life from outward evil free,
    From every gross enormity,
        Her life of nature was.
    Harmless she passed her *time to play,*
    Stranger to Christ, the living way,
        Regardless of his cross.

---

2. *FH* 1759, 49–59.

4. But when she heard the Gospel sound,
  The seed received in the good ground,
    The heart-engrafted word,
  Produced an hundred-fold increase,
  And, joined to Jesu's witnesses,
    She gloried in *her* Lord.

5. With joy she flew her all to sell,
  Borne on the wings of rapid zeal,
    Impatient of delay;
  Away she cast, with eager strife,
  Kindred, and friends, and more than life,
    She cast her fame away.

6. Where Satan keeps his gaudy throne,
  Firm as the righteous Lot, alone
    Against the world she stood,
  The cross endured, the shame despised,
  And only sought, and only prized,
    The praise that comes from God.

7. When men and fiends against her rose,
  Could all her fierce opprobrious foes
    Her steadfast faith o'erturn?
  A follower of the patient Lamb,
  The hatred she with love o'ercame,
    And triumphed in the scorn.

8. Her solid piety unfeigned,
  A witness from her foes obtained,
    And forced them to confess,
  "Where faith appears with virtue crowned,
  Religion pure on earth is found,
    And all her paths are peace."

Part II

1. Long in those peaceful, pleasant ways
    She walked, she ran the Christian race,
    With *never-slackening* care;
    Studious her talent to improve,
    She lived a life of faith and love,
    Of holiness and prayer.

2. The weightier matters of the law
    With single eye she clearly saw,
    Nor overlooked the less:
    Her tithe of mint she gladly paid,
    But the main stress on mercy laid,
    And truth and righteousness.

3. The golden rule she still pursued,
    And did to others as she would
    Others should do to her:
    Justice composed her upright soul,
    Justice did all her thoughts control,
    And formed her character.

4. Her morals, O thou bleeding Lamb,
    Forth from that open fountain came,
    That wounded side of thine;
    Thy love of equity she caught,
    Thy Spirit in her spirit wrought
    The righteousness divine.

5. Thenceforth an Israelite indeed,
   By child-like innocency led,
      And ignorant of art,
   She her integrity approved,
   To God and man; the truth she loved,
      And spoke it from her heart.

6. To falsehood an eternal foe,
   The fair pretense, the specious show,
      The gross and colored lie;
   Darkness she never put for light,
   Evil for good, or wrong for right,
      Or fraud for piety.

7. Through all her words the soul within,
   The honest, artless soul, was seen,
      Ingenuous, pure, and free;
   Candor and love were sweetly joined
   With easy nobleness of mind,
      And true simplicity.

8. Inspired with godliness sincere,
   She had her conversation here,
      No guile in her was found:
   Cheerful and open as the light,
   She dwelt in her own people's sight,
      And gladdened all around.

Part III

1. Mercy, that heaven-descending guest,
   Resided in her gentle breast,
      And full possession kept;
   While listening to the orphan's moan,
   And echoing back the widow's groan,
      She wept with them that wept.

2. Affliction, poverty, disease,
   Drew out her soul in soft distress,
     The wretched to relieve:
   In all the works of love employed,
   Her sympathizing soul enjoyed
     The blessedness to give.

3. Her Savior in his members seen,
   A stranger she received him in,
     An hungry Jesus fed,
   Tended her sick, imprisoned Lord,
   And flew in all his wants to'afford
     Her ministerial aid.

4. A nursing-mother to the poor,
   For them she husbanded her store,
     Her life, her all, bestowed;
   For them she labored day and night,
   In doing good her whole delight,
     In copying after God.

5. But did she then herself conceal
   From her own flesh? or kindly feel
     Their every want and woe?
   'Tis Corban *this,* she never said;
   But dealt alike her sacred bread,
     To feed both friend and foe.

6. Free from the busy worldling's cares,
   Who gathers riches—for his heirs,
     Who hoards what God hath given;
   Fast as the Lord her basket blessed,
   Fast as her well-got wealth increased,
     She laid it up in heaven.

7. Witness, ye servants of the Lord,
   Ye Preachers of the joyous word,
      Constrained with her t' abide:
   With Lydia's open house and heart,
   Glad of her carnal things t' impart,
      She all your wants supplied.

8. Surely ye judged her faithful *then;*
   And did she not through life remain
      Invariably the same?
   Her even soul to heaven aspired,
   The only mind of Christ desired,
      The tempers of the Lamb.

Part IV

1. Though envy foul its poison shed,
   To blast the venerable dead,
      With base reproach to load,
   She did not lose her pious pains;
   Her judgment with her Lord remains,
      Her work is with her God.

2. She never left her former love,
   Her zeal, or boldness to reprove
      Triumphant wickedness:
   Since first she knew the Crucified,
   She never cast her shield aside,
      Or forfeited her peace.

3. Constant, unwarped from first to last,
   She kept the faith, and held it fast,
      From sin and error free,
   Contending for the faith *alone,*
   The name inscribed in the white stone,
      The *life* of piety.

4. While others spent their strength for naught,
   For trifles she no longer fought,
       For *human* rules or rites;
   Her soul the *Shibboleths* disdained,
   By rigid novices maintained,
       And smooth-tongued hypocrites.

5. With ease her quick-discerning eyes
   Looked through the *soft* and thin disguise,
       The *meek* and *humble* veil:
   Beneath the *superficial* grace,
   She knew the lurking fiend to trace,
       The rage and pride of hell.

6. Yet neither earth nor hell could move
   Her firm, unconquerable love
       To Jesus and his flock:
   Her faith did all assaults endure,
   And stood, like its foundation sure,
       Established on a rock.

7. She loved, but leaned no more on man,
   A broken reed, an helper vain;
       People and Ministers,
   Men of like passions, she beheld,
   Their faults and weaknesses concealed,
       And helped them by her prayers.

8. Their Master she revered in them,
   With grateful love, and high esteem,
       Rejoiced their work to own;
   But only Christ *her Lord* allowed,
   And with entire devotion bowed
       To Jesu's name alone.

Part V

1. Free from the partial blind respect,
   Which marks the favorite of a sect,
       Implicitly resigned;
   With *others'* eyes she scorned to see,
   And stretched her arms of charity,
       Ingrasping humankind.

2. In love and every grace she *grew,*
   As nearer her departure drew;
       The active, restless soul
   From strength to greater strength went on,
   Swifter and swifter still she run,
       To reach the heavenly goal.

3. She lived a burning, shining light,
   With never-fading luster bright,
       With never-cooling love:
   Meet for the infinite reward,
   Expecting to receive her Lord
       And Bridegroom from above.

4. He came, and warned her to depart,
   He knocked at her attentive heart,
       And fitted for the sky;
   She opened to her welcome Guest,
   With eager, instantaneous haste
       She then got up, to die.

5. *To die,* her only business then,
    The meed of all her toils to gain,
        Made ready long before,
    She flies to lay her body down,
    And pain, and sin, and grief are gone,
        And suffering is no more.

6. "Nothing," she cries, "can shake my peace,
    My body or my soul distress,
        Or tempt me once to fear;
    My full salvation is wrought out,
    I cannot mourn, I cannot doubt,
        For Christ and heaven are here.

7. "Not in my helpless self I trust,
    But on my faithful Lord and just
        In life and death depend;
    Secure of everlasting bliss,
    Into those gracious hands of His
        My spirit I commend."

8. She speaks, and bows her willing head,
    She sinks among th' immortal dead,
        Without a lingering groan;
    Meek, as the Lamb of God, departs,
    And carries up our bleeding hearts
        To that eternal throne.

Part VI

1. There with the virgin-choir she sits,
   And Jesus her appeal admits
      From earth's unrighteous bar:
   He kept her faithful unto death,
   And with a never-fading wreath
      Rewards his servant there.

2. Go, envious fiend, and force her down;
   Go, pluck the jewels from her crown,
      And lessen her reward:
   Pollute by thy opprobrious praise,
   Or tear her from that blissful place,
      Or part her from her Lord.

3. The sacrilegious hope is vain
   Her spotless purity to stain,
      Her heavenly joy t' impair;
   The saint, whom erring saints disown,
   Shall smile on a superior throne,
      And brighter glories wear.

4. Yes, happy soul, so closely pressed
   On earth, in heaven, to Jesu's breast,
      With him thou reign'st above;
   Beyond our censure, or our praise,
   Enthroned where purest seraphs gaze,
      In all the heights of love.

5. How far below thy dazzling sphere
    Shall all thy blushing foes appear,
        If finally forgiven!
    O might thy censurers, and I,
    Obtain the grace, like thee, to die,
        And kiss thy feet in heaven.

6. Savior, regard my vehement prayer,
    Who only canst my loss repair,
        And solid comfort send;
    Send down thy likeness from above,
    And, in that spirit of meekest love,
        O give me back my friend!

7. I loved her for thy sake alone,
    For on her soul thine image shone;
        Ah! wouldst thou, Lord, impress
    The heavenly character on mine,
    And fill my heart with peace divine,
        And joy and righteousness!

8. O might I of thy follower learn
    The calm and genuine unconcern
        For human praise or blame,
    The patient faith, the even mind,
    The love unconquerably kind,
        The meekness of the Lamb!

9. I want—to love my foes, like her,
    Nor shrink from Satan's messenger,
        Nor turn my face aside;
    But silently enjoy the loss,
    The shame, the wrong, and hug the cross
        With Jesus crucified.

10. I want (alas, thou know'st my heart!)
      As safe and sudden to depart,
          As meet thy face to see;
      I groan my happier friend t' o'ertake,
      And give my gasping spirit back,
          And die like her—and thee.

CHAPTER 9

Anne Wigginton

d. April 24, 1757

One encounters a Mr. and Mrs. Wigginton as early as 1739 in Charles Wesley's *Journal*. On a number of occasions, Charles accompanies Mr. Wigginton on horseback. He records that on Sunday, September 16, 1739, he "took coach at six with Mr and Mrs Wigginton, Lucretia Smith, and Mrs Grevil, for Hanham-Mount."[1] There Charles preached to between three and four thousand. On October 26 of that year, he baptized Mr. Wigginton at Baptist-Mills.[2] He records another encounter at Mr. Wigginton's on November 1, 1739.[3]

Mr. Wiggtinton died before his wife, Anne, who once lost a child, a son, perhaps at childbirth or at least soon after birth. The death of her loved ones did not rob her, however, of faith and a life filled with righteous works. She was not a person of pretense, rather "Showed her faith by humble fear" (Part I, 2:6). Her good deeds were not for show, but revealed her "reverence for the things of God" (Part I, 3:3). As so often emphasized by Wesley, "patient love" (Part I, 3:6) characterized her nature.

She lived a "pattern to believers" (Part I, 6:3) that is often what Wesley discloses in his death poems in praise of the lives of the saints; namely she was

1. *MS Journal*, 1:198.
2. *MS Journal*, 1:217.
3. *MS Journal*, 1:219.

Possessed by Mary's better part,

And Martha's hands, and Lydia's heart. (Part I, 6:5–6)

She was an embodiment of the best strengths of all three women, the "Martha-Mary Formula" mentioned earlier.

The life pattern she lived is filled with wise counsel for others, according to Wesley.

(1) She was not a boaster, especially of faith she had not tried.

(2) She was a self-effacing woman, for "Her own good deeds she could not see" (Part I, 7:3). She was not a conscious good-deed-doer. She apparently did works of goodness for their sake and that of others, not her own. Even as she approached death, she did not look back upon good accomplished but "Complained, 'She never yet begun'" (Part I, 7:6).

(3) She grasped the frailty of human nature and knew such frailty characterized her own existence.

(4) She knew "that agony of love unknown" (Part II, 3:5) through the loss of a son, yet was strengthened by such agony, rather than defeated by it. She knew, as only a mother knows, the joy and pain of the lengthy travail for the life of a child—the months of anticipation and hope for new life—only to have all end in the death of the longed-for child. Just as she is the mother of the soul in life, she is its mother in death—a perception of the human participation in the gift of life, which is often forgotten.

(5) She had a vision of God revealed in Christ that sustained her in life and death. Here we find one of Wesley's most eloquently stated perceptions of the Christian's hope in death. The eyes of faith help one to focus the vision—the vision of plunging into the depth of God. What greater joy can there be?

Like Moses on the mountain laid
   With longing looks, and ravished eyes,
She sees the Savior's arms displayed;
   She sees his open face, and dies!
Drops at his kiss the mortal clod,
And plunges in the depths of God. (Part II, 8:1–6)

On the Death of Mrs. Anne Wigginton,[4]
April 24th, 1757

Part I

1. What shall we say? It is the Lord!
       His name be praised, his will be done!
    Bereaved by his revoking word,
       We meekly render him his own,
    And faultless mourn our partner fled,
    Our friend removed, our Dorcas dead.

2. A Christian good, without pretense,
       A widow by her works approved,
    A saint indeed is summoned hence,
       To triumph with her Best-beloved,
    In whom she found acceptance here,
    And *showed* her faith by humble fear.

3. By works of righteousness she showed
       The gracious principle within,
    By reverence for the things of God,
       By deadness to the world and sin,
    By laying up her wealth above,
    By all the toils of patient love.

4. *FH* 1759, 248–51.

4. Memorial of her faith unfeigned,
     As incense sweet, before the throne,
   Did not her prayers and alms ascend,
     And bring the heavenly herald down?
   Did she not for the Preacher call,
   With news of pardoning grace for all?

5. What though she in the desert pined,
     And languished for the light in vain,
   Her soul, obedient and resigned,
     Did darkly safe with God remain,
   Who led the trembling servant on,
   And blessed her in a path unknown.

6. Unconscious of the grace received,
     She mourned, as destitute of grace,
   A pattern to believers lived,
     And labored on with even pace,
   Possessed by Mary's better part,
   And Martha's hands, and Lydia's heart.

7. No noisy self-deceiver she,
     No boaster vain of faith untried:
   Her own good deeds she could not see,
     But wrought, and cast them all aside;
   And, when her glorious race was run,
   Complained, "I've never yet begun."

Part II

1. Soon as the warning angel came,
      That called her up to worlds on high,
   Meek as a death-devoted lamb,
      Yet starting, as unfit to die,
   Her nature's frailty she confessed,
   And sunk upon her Savior's breast.

2. He owned the soul so dearly loved,
      And, cutting short his work of grace,
   Her sins insensibly removed,
      Made meet at once to see his face;
   And lo! her latest fears are o'er,
   And pain and suffering are no more.

3. One only labor yet remains,
      Her genuine faith to justify,
   One only care the spirit detains,
      When winged, and ready for the sky:
   That agony of love unknown,
   That cry in death, "My son, my son!"

4. Can she her sucking child forget,
      In travail for his soul so long?
   Discharging nature's double debt,
      She warns him with a faltering tongue;
   She wins him by her latest breath,
   The mother of his soul in death.

5. By all the powers of love pursued,
        To Christ with holy violence driven,
    She claims him for the Savior-God,
        She turns and lifts his heart to heaven:
    In faith's almighty arms she bears,
    And crowns her counsels with her prayers.

6. In vain her strength and language fail,
        Speechless she urges her request,
    She *will* with the God-Man prevail:
        And now of all her wish possessed,
    Smiling, she looks him back the praise,
    And heaven is opened in her face.

7. Those heavenly smiles distinctly tell
        The rapturous bliss her spirit feels,
    The glorious joy unspeakable,
        Which Christ to dying saints reveals;
    The sight which none can here conceive,
    The sight which none can see and live.

8. Like Moses on the mountain laid
        With longing looks, and ravished eyes,
    She sees the Savior's arms displayed,
        She sees his open face, and dies!
    Drops at his kiss the mortal clod,
    And plunges in the depths of God.

CHAPTER 10

Mrs. Hannah Dewal

[d. November 12, 1762]

Hannah Dewal is often named in Charles Wesley's correspondence and *Journal*.[1] Her last years were lived at The Limes, which was sold to her by the banker Ebenezer Blackwell when its owner, Mrs. Jane Sparrow, died. Blackwell was the executor of her estate. Soon thereafter, Blackwell bought back a large share of the manor, which became the residence of his family. However, Mrs. Dewal continued to live there.

The Wesley brothers often went to The Limes for rest, where John often focused on publishing endeavors. Thus, they became very well acquainted with Mrs. Sparrow, Mrs. Dewal, and the Blackwell family. Before his marriage to Sarah Gwynne, Charles consulted both Sparrow and Dewal on the wisdom of such a union. Mrs. Dewal is frequently mentioned with Elizabeth Blackwell, wife of the banker, and both are held in high esteem by Charles and his wife, Sally. They were considered to be faithful servants of God in the circle of the Methodist societies.

In his poem dedicated to Hannah Dewal, Charles suggests that one should dwell on her memory because of what she bequeathes us: genuine faith, tempered zeal, noble intellect, a free mind, and diligence in searching the word. She fixed her eyes on God and walked a steady path.

The Wesleys often stressed the wedding of mind, heart, and hands in their interpretation of what it means to follow Christ. A

1. *MS Journal*, 2:531, 595.

life that pursues such a holistic blending of God's gifts is characterized by constancy, patience, transparency, friendship, humble confidence, and love. All of these Charles Wesley finds in Hannah Dewal.

Constancy—She was subject to:

> No sudden fits of transient love,
> No instantaneous starts she knew. (Part I, 5:1–2)

So steadfast was she in her pilgrimage of faith that she dreamed no shallow dreams of wealth, but was content to sacrifice substance for matters of the heart and hence became poor.

Self-effacement—Her commitment to God was so strong that her service was unconscious. She did not know how God's work grew and did not try to explain it.

Patience—Hannah Dewal was not compelled by "Now" (the immediate present), but recognized the need to wait upon the Lord and, hence, to be renewed by God's mind.

Transparency—She was who she was and had nothing to hide.

> Careful to be, and not be seen,
> Whate'er she was, she was to God. (Part I, 6:3–4)

This enabled her to live above pride, wrath, and fear.

Compassion—In spite of her own suffering, she was compassionate.

> Soft pity filled her generous breast,
> And mixed the eagle with the dove. (Part I, 7:5–6)

Friendship—This was her constant demeanor. She was able to love others fully and embraced a friend with "love entire" (Part I, 8:5). Wesley says that those who knew her shared life with an angel. The delight of her soul was to impart joy, to oblige, and to please. Therefore, he asks, "Was ever friendship more divine" (Part I, 9:8)?

Openness—What magnitude of heart characterized Hannah Dewal! She took the world into her heart, because she had experienced God's grace, namely the outpouring of God's love in the gift of the Savior's loving life on her behalf.

> The world into her heart she takes
> The purchase dear of Jesu's blood. (Part II, 1:7)

Love—Great love filled her life and inspired humble confidence and kind counsel.

> When language failed, her silence spoke
> In meekest majesty of love. (Part II, 9:1–2)

All of this is the memory that Hannah Dewal bequeaths to us and that Charles Wesley would have us constantly recall, so that we might follow her pattern of living.

On the Death of Mrs. Hannah Dewal[2]

Part I

1. Farewell, thou best of friends, farewell;
      (Since God revokes the richest loan;)
   Return, with kindred souls to dwell,
      As pure and upright as thine own.
   No longer could our prayers detain
      The pilgrim from her heavenly rest:
   Go, blessed saint, with Jesus reign,
      And lean for ever on his breast.

2. In hope to share thine happiness,
      We check the' unruly, selfish sigh,

2. Published posthumously in *PW*, 6:318–23. There exist two manuscript drafts of Wesley's hymn for Hannah Dewal, with a considerable number of variant readings. See both drafts titled "MS Death of Hannah Dewal" on the website of *CSWT*: http://divinity.duke.edu/sites/divinity.duke.edu/files/documents/cswt/42_MS_Death_of_Hannah_Dewal.pdf.

Restraining nature's soft excess,
    The tears commanding from our eye.
When Jesus to himself doth take
    A vessel of God's glorious love,
'Tis sacrilege to wish her back,
    To rob the sanctuary above.

3. Yet should we on her memory dwell,
    The pattern fair she left behind,
Her genuine faith and tempered zeal,
    Her noble, free, Berean mind;
Her diligence to search the word,
    "If one's own pardoned sin may know;"
She sought till there she found her Lord,
    And held and never let him go.

4. On God she fixed her single eye,
    And steady in God's steps went on,
Studious by works to testify
    The power of God in weakness shown.
A quiet follower of the Lamb,
    She walked in whom she had received,
And more and more showed forth God's name,
    And more and more like Jesus lived.

5. No sudden fits of transient love,
    No instantaneous starts, she knew;
But showed her heart was fixed above,
    And poorer still and poorer grew.
The seed increased, she knew not how,
    Nor aimed her Savior's work t' explain,
Nor tempted him by nature's Now,
    But waited all his mind to gain.

6. Transparent as the crystal stream,
       Her life in even tenor flowed;
    Careful to be, and not to seem,
       Whate'er she was, she was to God.
    Superior to reproach and praise,
       By no fantastic impulse driven,
    As unperceived she ran her race,
       As rapid as the orbs of heaven.

7. Thither her God-like spirit soared,
       Above all pride, all wrath, all fear;
    She triumphed with her glorious Lord,
       Yet suffered with his members here.
    At every shape of woe distressed,
       How did her yearning bowels move!
    Soft pity filled her generous breast,
       And mixed the eagle with the dove.

8. For friendship formed, her constant heart
       With pure, intense affection glowed;
    She could not give her friend a part,
       Because she gave the whole to God.
    Her friend she clasped with love entire,
       Enkindled at the Savior's throne,
    A spark of that celestial fire,
       A ray of that eternal Sun.

9. Could actions, words, or looks express
       How warm, how boundless, her esteem?
    Her soul's delight to' oblige and please,
       Bliss to impart her joy supreme.
    Say you, who shared that angel here,
       Whom neither life nor death disjoin,

Was ever transport more sincere,
    Was ever friendship more divine?

Part II

1.   Celestial charity expands
    The heart to all our ransomed race;
Though knit to one in closest bands,
    Her soul doth every soul embrace.
She no unkind exception makes,
    A childlike follower of her God;
The world into her *heart* she takes,
    The purchase dear of Jesu's blood.

2.   She loved even that most straightened sect
    Who every other sect disown,
Who all beside themselves reject,
    As heaven were bought for them alone:
With noble frankness she confessed
    Good out of Babylon might come,
And cherished in her candid breast
    The warmest partisan of Rome.

3.   But, numbered with the British sheep,
    She prized and held the blessing fast,
Resolved her privilege to keep,
    Till all the storms of life were past:
She kept the faith at first received,
    (Nor fiercely judged who turned aside,)
A daughter of our Zion lived,
    A mother of our Israel died.

4. Warned of her dissolution near,
   By waning strength and lingering pain,
   She blessed the welcome messenger;
   (To live was Christ, to die was gain;)
   Made ready for her heavenly Lord,
   Who came God's servant to release,
   Her lamp with holiness was stored,
   Her spirit kept in perfect peace.

5. She cast the tempting fiend behind,
   Who preached, in her last sacred hours,
   "Now, now believe again, and find
   Sensations new and rapturous powers."
   In vain to instantaneous pride
   He urged a saint of Christ possessed;
   With ease she turned the dart aside,
   And closer clave to Jesu's breast.

6. Her humble confidence she held,
   Built on a Rock that could not move,
   And, conscious of her pardon sealed,
   And filled with purity of love,
   The world with wide-spread arms embraced,
   Partaker of her Savior's mind,
   And, dying, all her soul confessed
   Alike drawn out to humankind.

7. Her convoy to those endless joys,
   While Israel's flaming guard attends,
   The precious moments she employs
   In dealing blessings to her friends;
   In counsels kind as each had need,
   In witnessing the truth of grace,
   While angels crowd around her bed,
   And heaven is opened in her face.

8. "My Master calls; at the command,
   Joyful I drop this earthly clod;
My roll I carry in my hand;
   'Tis written, signed, and sealed with blood:
"My way," she cries, "is strewed with flowers;
   A pleasant path before me lies,
And leads to amaranthine bowers,
   And leads to Christ in paradise."

9. When language failed, her silence spoke
   In meekest majesty of love;
On opening heaven she fixed her look,
   Like angels worshipping above:
Full of unutterable awe,
   Her look th' Invisible declared,
As bringing, in the sight she saw,
   Her weighty crown, her vast reward.

10. That vision of the One in Three
   Sweetly dissolves the human shrine,
It swallows up mortality,
   In joy ineffably divine:
That sight, too strong for life to bear,
   Her true eternal life displays,
And, eagle-like, she cleaves the air,
   And mingles with the Glorious Blaze.

CHAPTER 11

Elizabeth Blackwell

d. March 27, 1772

Elizabeth Blackwell was, as previously noted, wife of Ebenezer Blackwell, the London banker whose country house was at Lewisham. They later lived at the manor, The Limes, first owned by Mrs. Jane Sparrow. Elizabeth was a frequent companion of the Wesleys and one whose presence and friendship was greatly valued by them.

Wesley begins his poem to Elizabeth Blackwell with a prayer, and asks that we may pursue the path she has walked in life until we come to her own view of existence, namely that we see God's glory in all things and become inspired by "tender, gracious awe" and "innocence and purity" (Part I, 2:5–6). Like her, he prays that we may travel the path of wisdom and serve our Maker day and night. This is what it means to be wholly lost in grace as she was. Perhaps this alone is the reason why she was able to embody two character traits that often seem mutually exclusive: self-sustained integrity and lowliness or humility.

Though she personally sought to be faithful to God's law, her life was not immured and directed to herself. To the contrary,

> Faithful even then, she flew to tend,
> > Where'er distressed, the sick and poor,
> Rejoiced for them her life to spend,
> > And all thy gifts through them restore. (Part I, 5:5–8)

The fulfillment of faith evoked the spending of her life for the distressed, sick, and poor. It is through such engagement of her whole being in the lives of these people, and through prayer, that she experienced God's Spirit in her life. She was imbued with meekness, and God's word was ingrafted in her heart. Elizabeth understood holistic living to mean the sole pursuit of God's love, which resulted in complete sanctification at death.

After the prayerful tribute to Elizabeth Blackwell in Part I, Wesley addresses in three succeeding parts her *attitude toward the Christian life* (Part II), *attitude toward others* (Part III), and *attitude toward death* (Part IV).

The attitude toward the Christian life that Wesley discovers in her life is one that is compelling through wisdom, peacefulness, and the meek Spirit of God. These three are the key to what shapes her own view of God's mission in her life.

> By wisdom pure and peaceable,
> By the meek Spirit of her Lord,
> She knows the stoutest to compel,
> And sinners wins without the word:
> They see the tempers of the Lamb,
> They feel the wisdom from above,
> And now, subdued to Jesu's name,
> As captives to resistless love. (Part II, 4:1–8)

What a powerful description of the incarnation of the gospel in an individual life. She so personified wisdom, peace, and meekness that others became "captives to resistless love" (Part II, 4:8). And she wins sinners without verbal proclamation: "And sinners wins without the word" (Part II, 4:4). Why? Because they "see" and "feel" (Part II, 4:5–6) in her the temper of Christ and the wisdom of God. They witness her humble walk with God, which is characterized by "Power, purity, and peace" (Part II, 6:8), and they encounter her living faith revealed in deeds:

> Her living faith by works was shown:
>> Through faith to full salvation kept,
> She made the sufferer's griefs her own,
>> And wept sincere with those that wept.
> Nursing the poor with constant care,
>> Affection soft, and heart-esteem,
> She saw her Savior's image there,
>> And gladly ministered to him. (Part II, 7:1–8)

Wesley begins his description of Elizabeth Blackwell's *attitude toward others* by stating that she was formed for friendship to secure the happiness of others.[1] She lived solely for others and the reclaiming of their lives for God. Her focus was not on her own happiness, but on that of others, yet in their happiness was her own. Hence, she embraced the whole world with love.

> So humble, affable, and meek,
>> Her gentle, inoffensive mind,
> None ever heard that angel speak
>> A railing speech, or word unkind. (Part III, 3:5–8)

Would that all people could be so described!

Her *attitude toward death* is simply stated by Wesley: "She welcomed death in Jesu's name" (Part IV, 1:3). What is there to fear from the God of truth and love? Nothing. He then couches in his own poetical paraphrase words like those he had heard her speak amid sickness and pain. What a transformation takes place, when one is so overwhelmed with the love of God!

> While in God's mercies I confide,
>> He keeps my soul in perfect peace;
> He comforts me on every side,
>> And pain is lost in thankfulness. (Part IV, 3:5–8)

What a faith posture for illness and death!

---

1. This is what Chilcote describes as "Holy Friendship" and says, "friendship mirrors the theological concern for accountable discipleship" (Chilcote, "Charles Wesley and Christian Practices," 45).

O that one might come to the end of life and have this tribute made by a friend or acquaintance:

> The witness which through life she bore,
>> When now made ready to ascend,
> Loving, and meek, resigned, and poor,
>> She bears consistent to the end:
> No sudden starts, with nature mixed,
>> No violent ecstasies of grace,
> Her eyes on God, her heart is fixed,
>> And silence speaks her Savior's praise. (Part IV, 7:1–8)

On the Death of Mrs. Elizabeth Blackwell
March 27, 1772[2]

1. God of all power, and truth, and love,
> Whose faithful mercies never end,
> Thy longing servant to remove,
> Who dost the flaming convoy send;
> Help us thine attributes to praise,
> Help us thy follower to pursue,
> Till all obtain the crowning grace,
> Till all with her thy glory view.

2. E'er yet she into being came,
> Thou didst thy favorite handmaid choose,
> Thy love inscribed her with thy name,
> And marked the vessel for thy use:
> With tender, gracious awe inspired,
> With innocence and purity,
> God, above all, the child desired,
> And gave her simple heart to thee.

2. See the the entry titled "MS Death of Elizabeth Blackwell" on the *CSWT* website: http://divinity.duke.edu/sites/divinity.duke.edu/files/documents/cswt/38 _MS_Death_of_Elizabeth_Blackwell.pdf. The poem also appears in an unfinished looseleaf draft: "MS Death of Elizabeth Blackwell." See also posthumous publication in *PW,* 6:323–31.

3. Her pious course with life began,
   Called by the consecrating rite,
In wisdom's pleasant paths she ran,
   And served her Maker day and night:
Watchful to keep her garments clean,
   Glad to frequent the hallowed place,
She never left her God for sin,
   Or *wholly* lost that earliest grace.

4. While, zealous for thy righteous law,
   She her integrity maintained,
Thou didst her trembling spirit awe,
   And blessed with lowliness unfeigned:
No pharisaic pride or scorn
   Could harbor in her bosom find,
Her virtue into poison turn,
   Or taint so pure and good a mind.

5. Touching the legal righteousness,
   While blameless in thy sight she lived,
Thee she confessed in all her ways,
   And all her good from thee received;
Faithful even then, she flew to tend,
   Where'er distressed, the sick and poor,
Rejoiced for them her life to spend,
   And all thy gifts through them restore.

6. Did not her alms and prayers arise,
   Memorial sweet, before thy throne?
Grateful, accepted sacrifice,
   They brought the Gospel-blessing down:
To One who thee sincerely feared,
   Thou didst the Comforter impart:
The herald spake; the grace appeared,
   And stamped salvation on her heart.

7. Her unopposing heart received,
       With meekness, the ingrafted word,
    With reverential joy believed,
       And sunk before her smiling Lord:
    Reciprocal affection moved,
       And wonder asked, "How can it be?
    Hath God so poor a creature loved,
       Or bought so mean a worm as me?"

Part II

1. Commences now the Christian race,
       The conflict good, the life concealed,
    Th' eternal God, replete with grace,
       Jesus is to her soul revealed:
    Translated into wondrous light,
       Humbly assured of sin forgiven,
    She goes in peace, she walks in white,
       And close pursues her Guide to heaven.

2. Exulting with her Head to rise,
       She seeks the things concealed above,
    For joy sells all, the jewel buys,
       The heavenly treasure of God's love;
    Jesus alone resolved to gain,
       And, crucified with Jesus here,
    The finished sanctity t' attain,
       The lowliness of filial fear.

3. Fear to offend or God or man
       In all her conversation shines,
    While following the Redeemer's plan
       She carries on his great designs:
    Watchful immortal souls to win,
       The God supreme she dares command,
    Constrains the outcasts to come in,
       And shows them their expiring Friend.

4. By wisdom pure and peaceable,
    By the meek Spirit of her Lord,
  She knows the stoutest to compel,
    And sinners wins without the word:
  They see the tempers of the Lamb,
    They feel the wisdom from above,
  And bow, subdued, to Jesu's name,
    As captives of resistless love.

5. Witness, ye once to evil sold!
    Witness her kind parental zeal,
  Thou wanderer of the Romish fold,
    Pursued so long, and loved so well!
  Saved by her prayers, through Jesu's blood,
    Thy endless debt make haste to pay;
  Go, meet her at the throne of God,
    Her crown and glory in that day.

6. Witness, ye souls to her allied,
    Her humble walk with God below;
  She ne'er looked back, or lost her Guide,
    Or started like a broken bow;
  She ne'er forsook her former love,
    Or wandered in the wilderness,
  But labored on her faith to prove
    By power, and purity, and peace.

7. Her living faith by works was shown:
    Through faith to full salvation kept,
  She made the sufferer's griefs her own,
    And wept sincere with those that wept:
  Nursing the poor with constant care,
    Affection soft, and heart-esteem,
  She saw her Savior's image there,
    And gladly ministered to him.

8. How did she entertain the spies,
  By fervent prayer their labors speed,
Bring down the Spirit's fresh supplies,
  And more than share their every deed!
To spread Jehovah's gracious word,
  To do God's will, her pleasant meat,
And serve the servants of her Lord,
  And wash an old disciple's feet!

Part III

1. For converse formed by art divine,
  For friendship delicate as pure,
Did she not all with ease resign,
  To make the others' bliss secure?
On them by heavenly grace bestowed,
  Her generous heart entire she gave;
And, charged with the behests of God,
  She only lived their souls to save.

2. As born her earthly lord to please,
  Studious of his content alone,
Dispersing virtuous happiness,
  She made her every wish her own
As in their heavenly Bridegroom's sight,
  The Church their vows with rapture pay,
Her duty ministered delight,
  Her joy and glory was t' obey.

3. God's image she in all revered,
  And honored all the ransomed race;
Thrice happy soul, who always feared,
  Whose love did the whole world embrace!
So humble, affable, and meek,
  Her gentle, inoffensive mind,
None ever heard that angel speak
  A railing speech, or word unkind.

4. Upright she walked in open day,
       Free as the light, on all she shone,
    In sight of God whose eyes survey
       The secret wish to all unknown:
    Whene'er her pleasing voice we heard,
       We saw her thoughts spontaneous rise,
    Whose heart in every word appeared,
       Whose generous soul abhorred disguise.

5. Even as life the heavenly flame
       In all her words and actions burned,
    While still, invariably the same,
       Her sweetness all estates adorned:
    Strangers with loving awe confessed
       The ministerial spirit below,
    And every charmed spectator blessed,
       And lived and died without a foe.

Part IV

1. Soon as th' appointed sickness came,
       And *promised* her departure near,
    She welcomed death in Jesu's name,
       Nor weakly dropped a lingering tear.
    Let those lament with conscious dread,
       Who teach, "Ye must in darkness die:"
    She knew her Advocate had sped;
       Her place was ready in the sky.

2. "How can I doubt my blissful end,
       How can I tremble to remove,
    When Jesus, my almighty Friend,
       Is the great God of truth and love?

Christ, God supreme for ever blest,
    Sole self-existing God, I own,
Who purchased my eternal rest,
    And calls me up to share the throne.

3. "Surrounded by his power I stand
      Whom day and night his mercies keep,
  He holds me in his chastening hand,
      He gives to his beloved sleep;
  While in his mercies I confide,
      He keeps my soul in perfect peace,
  He comforts me on every side,
      And pain is lost in thankfulness.

4. "Who for so poor a creature care,
      My friends are with his kindness kind;
  My burdens for his sake they bear;
      The Fountain in the stream I find:
  I magnify my Saviour's name,
      I praise him with my parting breath,
  And, sinking into dust, proclaim
      The everlasting arms beneath."

5. In words like these the dying saint
      Her humble confidence expressed,
  Or calmly sighed her only want,
      And languished for that endless rest:
  Rest after toil and pain, how sweet
      To souls whose full reward is sure;
  Who their last wish, like her, submit,
      Like Jesus, to the end endure!

6. Enduring, with that patient Lamb,
     Th' appointed years of sacred woe,
   She comes as gold out of the flame,
     To triumph o'er her mortal foe:
   Sweet peace, and pure celestial hope,
     And humble joy, the bride prepare,
   While, waiting to be taken up,
     She whispers soft her final prayer.

7. The witness which through life she bore,
     When now made ready to ascend,
   Loving, and meek, resigned, and poor,
     She bears consistent to the end;
   No sudden starts, with nature mixed,
     No violent ecstasies of grace,
   Her eye on God, her heart is fixed,
     And silence speaks her Savior's praise.

8. Exempt from nature's agonies,
     Who now is able to conceive
   What with her closing eyes she sees?
     She cannot bear the sight and live:
   In sweet communion with her God,
     She glides insensibly away,
   Quietly drops the smiling clod,
     And mingles with eternal day!

CHAPTER 12

Hannah Butts

[d. 1762]

Hannah Butts was born Hannah Witham (b. 1720). Her parents, Thomas and Elizabeth, were active members of the Methodist Society in London. Hannah married Thomas Butts, also a member of the same Methodist Society, in 1746. He is mentioned a number of times in Charles's *MS Journal* as having accompanied John and Charles on several preaching events in the 1740s. Thomas Butts is well-known as the steward of the Wesley Book Room in London during the years 1753–1759.

Of the four known poems by Charles Wesley about her, published posthumously by George Osborn,[1] two are discussed here.

Wesley once again weeps for himself and others who no longer enjoy the presence of a saint, Hannah Butts, "who weeps no more" (Part I, 1:1). Very early in her life she was "called to seek a hidden God" (Part I, 3:2). She was guided by parents who apparently motivated her to follow God's commands. Interestingly Charles describes her as

1. See *PW,* 6:331–38. See also *MS FH,* "On the Death of Mrs Hannah Butts," 33–41, and *MS FH,* "On Being Desired," 32–33, on the website of the *CSWT.*

> One of those distinguished few
>> From their childhood sanctified,
> Washed by Christ, she never knew
>> When the blood was first applied. (Part I, 4:1–4)

She personified a redeemed and holy life from childhood and youth, which Wesley depicts in a three-part poem.

He begins by seeing her beyond death, in union with God, and looking back on earth and bidding all to follow the path she has trod, which has led her to God. If we are to aspire "after her" (Part I, 2:7), how are we to shape our lives? Wesley says, by aspiring to the qualities he sees in Hannah Butts.

Clearly, she knows who she is, has a healthy self-image, has no identity crisis, and lives with purpose.

(1) *She lived by cheerful obedience.*

> In the morning of her day,
>> Called to seek a hidden God,
> Cheerful she pursued her way,
>> In the paths of duty trod. (Part I, 3:1–4)

(2) *She loved in deed and truth.*

> Silent follower of the Lamb,
>> Him in deed and truth she loved. (Part I, 5:1–2)

Faith was not limited to the realm of doctrinal assertions, for "She her faith in actions showed."

(3) *She was humble and meek,* who did not esteem herself more than others. These qualities enabled her to be a gifted listener. It did not bother her not to be "the first" or "number one"; rather she was "Glad to be accounted least."

> Humble like the Lord, and meek,
>> Did she not herself abase?
> Swift to hear, and slow to speak,
>> Still she chose the lowest place,

> Glad to be accounted least;
>> Each she to herself preferred,
> Far beyond her fellows blessed,
>> Always blessed who always feared. (Part I, 6:1–8)

Wesley has an unusual vision of the humble and meek, which he sees personified in Hannah Butts, namely, the deeds of such persons are the "Wisest, virtuousest, best."

> Simple love, and lowly fear,
>> Kept possession of her breast,
> Made her every act appear
>> Wisest, virtuousest, best. (Part II, 4:5–8)

(4) *She served God in common tasks and simple things.*

> Daily she fulfilled God's word,
> In her meanest services
>> Ministering unto the Lord. (Part II, 2:2–4)

(5) *She exemplified the balance of active faith and contemplation described by Charles Wesley once again in the "Martha-Mary Formula."*

> Walking in her house with God,
>> Portioned with the better part,
> She her faith by actions showed,
>> Martha's hand and Mary's heart. (Part II, 1:1–4)

(6) *She rejected haughtiness and claims of instantaneous sanctification.* She saw the futility of those who bragged about their own perfection, who claimed that they had experienced instantaneous security and knew that of the chosen race, they were the "choicest." They had been made completely pure or holy all at once!

> Sinners she with pity saw
>> Of their own perfection proud,
> Pleased the public eye to draw,
>> Forward, turbulent, and loud,

> Witnesses of their own grace,
> "Instantaneously secure,
> "Choicest of the chosen race,
> "Pure at once, entirely pure!" (Part II, 1:1–8)

In the next stanza, we learn that she turned away calmly from such claims. Also, she did not judge them, but occupied herself with humble demeanor. She was neither proud nor bitter about such behavior. What did she do in the face of those who made such claims? "Studying to be quiet, still, / Still she kept her love and peace."

> Calm from such she turned away;
> Left them to their God unknown,
> Them to judge she could not stay,
> Busied with herself alone;
> Free from proud, or bitter zeal,
> Nature's wild or fierce excess,
> Studying to be quiet, still,
> Still she kept her love and peace. (Part II, 2:1–8)

(7) *She was a wise parent,* who displayed an unusual quality as a parent, namely gentle discipline. She did not blindly impose her will on her children; rather:

> Gently she their will inclined,
> Diligent her house to build,
> Wisely, rationally kind,
> With divine discretion filled:
> Far removed from each extreme,
> Conscious why her babes were given,
> Heirs of bliss, she lived for them,
> Lived to train them up for heaven. (Part II, 3:1–8)

(8) *She had the mind of Christ.* She heeded St. Paul's admonition, "Let this mind be in you, which was also in Christ Jesus," for she was "Blessed with Jesus' quiet mind" (Part II, 4:2).

(9) *She lived for others.* Because she was "Born that others might rejoice," she impacted their lives in diverse ways. She beguiled their cares through sweetness, and her melodious voice hushed grief and made anguish smile. A mere glance from her would scatter clouds.

> Born that others might rejoice,
> Sweetly she their cares beguiled;
> Listening to her tuneful voice,
> Grief was hushed, and anguish smiled:
> Clouds she scattered with her eye,
> Welcome as the peaceful dove;
> Vanquished by her soft reply,
> Nabal[2] melted into love. (Part III, 1:1–8)

(10) *She bore grief with integrity and confidence and faced death with assurance.* The meaning of existence for her was summarized in her own confession: "It is the Lord" (Part III, 2:8). Hence, she could lay all her grief at the Redeemer's feet, knowing that Christ is the "Messenger of lasting peace" (Part III, 4:5). With such faith, death becomes life.

> Life is to her rescue come,
> In her mortal pangs sustain;
> By the fruit of Mary's womb,
> She the full salvation gains. (Part III, 6:1–4)

Death is then a loving act. Indeed, Hannah Butts so personified divine love that her death is understood by Wesley as being effected by love. What an amazing thought, and what an outstanding tribute he pays her in these concluding lines:

> Heaven expanded in her heart,
> Love ineffable, divine,
> Makes the soul and body part,
> Swells and bursts the earthly shrine. (Part III, 7:1–4)

---

2. 1 Sam 25:2.

May She Have a Word with You?

On Being Desired to Write an Elegy
For Mrs. Hannah Butts[3]

1. Can I describe a worth like thine,
    Transcript of excellence divine,
    Though friendship urge, and love demand,
    The tribute of so mean a hand?
    Thy loveliness from far I see,
    Thy height of Christian dignity,
    But fail to utter *that* thou art,
    Or show thine image in my heart.

2. Could I like rapid Young aspire,
    Transported on his car of fire,
    Or flow with academic ease,
    Smooth as our own Isocrates,[4]
    Beautiful words I could not find
    Expressive of so fair a mind;
    But want an angel's tongue to paint
    The glories of an humble saint.

3. O were they all on me bestowed,
    The form and lineaments of God,
    God's image on thy soul impressed,
    God's love that filled thy faithful breast!
    How gladly then would I ascend
    With thee, to view our heavenly Friend;
    In rapturous strains God's praise repeat,
    And sing triumphant at thy feet!

3. *MS FH*, 32, *CSWT*. Published posthumously in *PW*, 6:331–32.
4. The Rev. James Hervey.

On the Death of Mrs. Hannah Butts[5]

Part I

1. Happy, pure, impassive soul!
    Ended are thy mournful days;
   She hath reached the heavenly goal,
    She hath won the glorious race,
   'Scaped out of the stormy deep,
    Angels welcome her to shore:
   For ourselves, alas, we weep,
    Not for her, who weeps no more.

2. Early from our vale of tears
    Snatched by her Redeemer's love,
   Ripe for God, she now appears
    With the spotless church above;
   Mixed with that triumphant choir,
    Still the pitying saint looks down,
   Bids us after her aspire,
    Win the fight, and claim the crown.

3. In the morning of her day,
    Called to seek a hidden God,
   Cheerful she pursued her way,
    In paths of duty trod,
   (Guided by parental hands,
    Stranger then to Christ her peace,)
   Ran the way of his commands,
    Followed after righteousness.

5. Published posthumously in *PW*, 6:335–38, except that stanzas 1 and 2 of Part II do not appear in either source. They are found in *UP*, 3:338.

4. One of those distinguished few
       From their childhood sanctified,
   Washed by Christ, she never knew
       When the blood was first applied;
   Favored of the Lord, and blessed,
       Nothing could his handmaid say,
   Only by her life confessed
       He had borne her sins away.

5. Silent follower of the Lamb,
       Him in deed and truth she loved,
   Prized the odor of his name,
       Never from his statutes roved,
   Tracked the footsteps of his flock,
       With his poor disciples stayed,
   Followed by their guardian Rock,
       Safe in God's almighty shade.

6. Humble, like the Lord, and meek,
       Did she not herself abase?
   Swift to hear, and slow to speak,
       Still she chose the lowest place,
   Glad to be accounted least;
       Each she to herself preferred,
   Far beyond her fellows blessed,
       Always blessed who always feared.

Part II

1. Sinners she with pity saw
      Of their own perfection proud,
   Pleased the public eye to draw,
      Forward, turbulent, and loud,
   Witnesses of their own grace,
      "Instantaneously secure,
   "Choicest of the chosen race,
      "Pure at once, entirely pure!"

2. Calm from such she turned away,
      Left them to their God unknown,
   Them to judge she could not stay,
      Busied with herself alone;
   Free from proud, or bitter zeal,
      Nature's wild or fierce excess,
   Studying to be quiet, still,
      Still she kept her love and peace.

3. Walking in her house with God,
      Portioned with the better part,
   She her faith by actions showed,
      Martha's hand and Mary's heart:
   Laboring on from morn to night,
      Still she offered up her care,
   Pleasing in her Savior's sight,
      Sanctified by faith and prayer.

4. Taught of God himself to please,
   Daily she fulfilled his word,
In her meanest services
   Ministering unto the Lord;
Happy if her constant smile
   Might but ease the sufferer's load,
Soften a companion's toil,
   Win her little ones to good.

5. Gently she their will inclined,
   Diligent her house to build,
Wisely, rationally kind,
   With divine discretion filled:
Far removed from each extreme,
   Conscious why her babes were given,
Heirs of bliss, she lived for them,
   Lived to train them up for heaven.

6. Principled with faith unfeigned,
   Blessed with Jesus' quiet mind,
Every part she well sustained,
   Bright in every function shined:
Simple love, with lowly fear,
   Kept possession of her breast,
Made her every act appear
   Wisest, virtuousest, best.

Part III

1. Born that others might rejoice,
    Sweetly she their cares beguiled;
Listening to her tuneful voice,
    Grief was hushed, and anguish smiled:
Clouds she scattered with her eye,
    Welcome as the peaceful dove;
Vanquished by her soft reply,
    Nabal melted into love.

2. More esteemed as nearer viewed,
    More beloved as longer known,
Good, without pretension good,
    Smooth and swift her race she run;
Patiently her soul possessed,
    When God's blessings she restored,
God in every stroke confessed,
    Meekly owned, "It is the Lord!"

3. Witness, her companions here,
    How she wailed her infants dead;
You who saw her tenderest tear,
    When her dearest comforts fled!
Did she not the murmurer shame,
    Teach the sufferer to submit,
Bless her great Redeemer's name,
    Weep in silence at his feet?

4. Smiling on his mourner there,
   Ready all her tears to dry,
Israel's Strength and Comforter
   Whispered her deliverance nigh:
Messenger of lasting peace,
   Pain, immortalizing pain,
Hastens to her soul's release,
   Gives her back her babes again.

5. Anguish if her Lord employs,
   Shall she not his choice approve?
Marked for everlasting joys,
   Summoned to her place above;
Happy in the arms of death,
   Lo! the heavenly victim lies,
Rachel gasping out her breath,
   Finishing her sacrifice!

6. Life is to her rescue come,
   In her mortal pangs sustains;
By the fruit of Mary's womb,
   She the full salvation gains:
Every promise is fulfilled,
   Every grace and blessing given;
Now the glorious heir is sealed,
   Ripe for all the joys of heaven.

7. Heaven expanded in her heart,
   Love ineffable, divine,
Makes the soul and body part,
   Swells and bursts the earthly shrine:
Wafted by th' angelic powers,
   In an ecstasy of praise,
To her Savior's arms she soars,
   Finds his throne, and sees his face!

CHAPTER 13

Mary Horton

d. May 4, 1786

Mary Durbin was born in 1752, eldest daughter of parents who became early participants in the work of the Wesleys in Bristol. Her father, Henry Durbin (ca. 1719–1799), was a trustee of the New Room chapel. When Charles and Sarah Wesley lived in Bristol, they became close friends with the Durbins.

John Wesley performed the wedding ceremony of Mary Durbin and John Horton on September 21, 1780. Mary's untimely death came during the sixth year of marriage, which occasioned Charles Wesley's lengthy poetical tribute to her. At first, he wrote a hymn and an epitaph, but revised the hymn in two additional drafts, expanding it to five parts in thirty-five stanzas of six lines each. The most polished version of the lengthy tribute is printed below.

Beginning in Part II of the poem, Wesley celebrates aspects of Mary Horton's life that are exemplary for all followers of Christ. (1) Her course of piety was so sincere and consistent that Charles recommends that everyone should spend the remainder of life in prayer and praise for her and remembering the course she followed while on earth.

Her walk with God, from which she never wavered, began in her youth. (2) The faithful discipline of her early years resulted in the wisdom of her later years. "Yet still she sighed for something more, / And sought she knew not what" (Part II, 5:5–6). Apparently, in some part of her life, she sought to justify herself by way of keeping of the law. But she was on a quest for something more, which she found in Jesus Christ.

As Wesley often did in his praise of women and their vibrant faith, he compares the woman he is extolling as possessing the virtues of three women mentioned in Scripture: Lydia, Mary, and Martha. Mary Horton came to faith as easily as Lydia believed— evidence once again of Wesley's use of the "Martha-Mary Formula." She received the seal of pardon with the joy of Mary, and "She ran the way of God's commands, / And ministered with Martha's hands" (Part II, 9:4–5). Her genuine faith was known by her works.

(3) Mary Horton's demeanor was exemplary, for she bore "the tempers of the Lamb" (Part III, 1:6). It was marked by sincerity and truth, and was free of fear and shame. How did she bear "the tempers of the Lamb?" She responded with compassion to the needy.

(4) She sought to aid those in distress, to speak a reconciling word, to embrace them with comfort, i.e., to pour in "the Balm of Gilead" (Part III, 3:4), especially for those who had been "bruised by sin" (Part III, 3:5). In doing these things, it became possible to "lead them to their Lord" (Part III, 3:6). "She poured out her heart" (Part III, 5:6) and was evidence of humble, active love, even in facing the death of her own children.

(5) By the way she lived, Mary Horton was an explanation of the mystery of union with Christ.

(6) She lived "every well-spent day" (Part IV, 2:5) as if it were her last. And facing her own death in no way diminished her love for God. "She could not doubt her Savior's love, / Or dread a stingless foe" (Part IV, 4:5–6).

In summary, the hallmarks of Mary Horton's life which should be a pattern of everyone's spiritual journey, are these:

(1) Be sincere and consistent on one's spiritual journey.

(2) Be an unwavering seeker in one's quest for the unknown, indeed for God.

(3) Let one's behavior be tempered by the behavior of Christ.

(4) Serve the poor and marginalized.

(5) Be an example of the mystery of oneness with Christ.

(6) Live every day as though it were the last, never diminishing one's love for God.

(7) Maintain a balance between active faith and contemplation.

On the Death of Mrs. Mary Horton
May 4, 1786, aged thirty-four years[1]

Part I

1. It is the Lord, whose will is done,
    He to the end hath loved his own,
        And now required his bride;
    Who went her mansion to prepare,
    Hath brought her home, his joy to share,
        And triumph at his side.

2. Her mourning days are finished soon,
    Her sun of life gone down at noon;
        But why should we complain,
    That Mercy hath abridged her years,
    And snatched her from our vale of tears,
        In endless bliss to reign?

3. To keep her here in vain we strove:
    She mounts! she claps her wings above!
        She grasps the glittering prize!
    In answer to our mended prayers,

1. Published posthumously in *PW,* 6:356–63. There are three drafts of this poem. See Charles Wesley's MS Verse, "MS Death of Mary Horton (Drafts 1, 2, & 3") on the website of the *CSWT.* The text printed here follows draft 3.

Enjoying, with salvation's heirs,
The life that never dies.

4. And can we now our loss regret,
Or wish to tear her from her seat,
Where high enthroned she sings?
No: rather let us strive t' increase
The cloud of Jesus' witnesses,
When death to glory brings.

5. Pursuing her, as she her Lord,
And laboring for a full reward,
Our friend we soon shall join;
The praise of *our* salvation give
To God that doth for ever live,
And to the Lamb divine.

5. Hastening the universal doom,
O wouldst thou, Lord, thy power assume,
And bring the kingdom down;
The number of thy saints complete,
And us, through patient faith made meet,
With joy eternal crown!

Part II

1. O that our residue of days
We all might spend in prayer, and praise
For our translated friend,
Contemplating her converse here,
Her course of piety sincere,
And her consistent end!

2. Her piety with life begun,
    Worshipper of the God unknown,
        She trembled and adored;
    Kept by her parents' hallowed cares,
    From sin, the world, and Satan's snares,
        And nurtured for the Lord.

3. Allured by his prevenient grace,
    Even she walked in pleasant ways,
        Far from the thoughtless crowd;
    A stranger to their hopes and fears,
    Remembering, in her tenderest years,
        Her Maker and her God.

4. In wisdom as in years she grew,
    Nor selfish guile, nor evil knew,
        Nor gay diversion's round;
    Like Eve in her Creator's sight,
    Her innocent and pure delight
        She in a garden found.

5. Her precious hours employing there
    In useful works, and praise, and prayer,
        She prized her happy lot:
    Her cup of earthly bliss run o'er,
    Yet still she sighed for something more,
        And sought she knew not what.

6. She knew not, till the God unknown
    Had drawn her, weary, to the Son,
        The Lord her righteousness;
    Who paid her ransom on the tree,
    From all iniquity to free,
        And save a world by grace.

7. Jesus beneath the fig-tree saw
    His handmaid, laboring by the law
        Herself to justify;
    And showed himself the way to God,
    And graciously the gift bestowed,
        Which she could never buy.

8. The harmless youth who freely loved,[2]
    He her sincerity approved,
        And touched her simple heart;
    She then with Lydia's ease believed,
    A pardon sealed with joy received,
        And Mary's better part.

9. Yet, though her choice was still to sit
    Delighted at the Master's feet,
        And listening to his word,
    She ran the way of God's commands,
    And ministered, with Martha's hands,
        To all that served her Lord.

10. Her genuine faith by works was known,
    Her light, with spreading luster, shone
        Impartial, unconfined;
    Her meat and drink God's will to do,
    And trace Christ's steps, and close pursue
        The Friend of human kind.

Part III

1. Say, ye companions of her youth,
    With what sincerity and truth,

2. See the Gospel of Mark 10:21.

How free from fear and shame,
Christ and his members she confessed,
And through a blameless life expressed
The tempers of the Lamb.

2. How did she put his bowels on,
And answer every plaintive groan
Of poverty and pain!
In sad variety of grief
The wretched sought from her relief,
Nor ever sought in vain.

3. She flew preventing their request,
To seek and succor the distressed,
The reconciling word,
The balm of Gilead to pour in,
Comfort and soothe the bruised by sin,
And lead them to their Lord.

4. Guide to her natural allies,
Endeared yet more by gracious ties,
She urged them on to show
Their faith by every righteous deed,
And close in all the steps to tread
Of God revealed below.

5. From those who did her Father's will,
A thought she knew not to conceal,
Incapable of art;
Blessed with a child's simplicity,
While, cheerful as the light and free,
She poured out all her heart.

6. When called the mystery to explain
    Of two in Christ, no longer twain,
        A figure of his bride,
    The meaning of the nuptial sign,
    The sacred ordinance divine,
        She showed exemplified.

7. To whom her plighted faith she gave,
    She with entire affection clave,
        Nor e'er resumed a part;
    Yet Jesus above all adored,
    Still rendering to her heavenly Lord
        An undivided heart.

8. When God, to prove her love sincere,
    A sacrifice than life, more dear,
        Did for her children call,
    Her children freely she resigned,
    Bereaved, yet happy still to find
        That Christ was all in all.

Part IV

1. She thus, adorning every state,
    Did with Christ's true disciples wait
        The Savior from above:
    Death could not find her off her guard,
    By prayer habitually prepared,
        By humble, active love.

2. Her life a testimony true
    That heaven was always in her view,

Till earthly scenes were past,
That here she had not long to stay,
Who lived as every well-spent day
Were destined for her last.

3.   Ready for her celestial home
Whene'er the messenger should come,
Her Lord was sure to find
His handmaid in his work employed,
Who long had given up all for God,
And cast the world behind.

4.   Unwarned of her release so near,
Insensible of pain or fear,
She needed not to know
The moment fixed for her remove;
She could not doubt her Savior's love,
Or dread a stingless foe.

5.   The tyrant was not worth a thought,
When Christ had her salvation wrought,
Had wholly sanctified;
When (half her race of glory run)
He sent Elijah's chariot down,
He came to fetch his bride.

6.   Like Moses caught to God's embrace,
Dissolved by God's *discovered* face,
Whom only she desired;
The race she in a moment won,
And calm, without a lingering groan,
In Jesus' sight expired.

7. Yet, mindful of her friends below,
      Stronger than death her love to show,
        By a divine decree,
      Indulged to comfort them that mourned,
      She stopped the flaming car, and turned,
        And shouted, "Victory!"

Part V

1. O God, who dost the victory give,
      The thanks of every heart receive,
        Through thy beloved Son,
      Who dost, for our Redeemer's sake,
      Vile, sinful souls vouchsafe to make
        The partners of thy throne.

2. The grace which saved our happy friend,
      Which made her faithful to the end,
        And decked her head with rays,[3]
      We shall for us sufficient prove,
      And strive, in humble fear and love,
        To perfect holiness.

3. Who did for her the kingdom buy,
      Jesus, for us went up on high,
        Our purchased thrones to claim;
      The same our Advocate with thee,
      The same our trust thy face to see,
        Through that almighty Name.

4. Father, we on that Name depend:
      Send, then, for us, the convoy send,

3. Author's italics added for emphasis.

For all with Jesus one;
Consummate us in heavenly bliss,
And by thy glorious saints increase
　　The glory of thy Son.

CHAPTER 14

Mary Stotesbury

d. March 17, 1759

In his *MS Journal,* Charles records on Thursday, June 7, 1750: "Carried Sally [his wife] to see our old friends at Newington Green. It is remarkable that the first time Mrs Stotesbury ever saw her, she said within herself, 'That person is to be my minister's wife.'"[1] As Charles and Sarah had only been married a little over a year at the time of Charles's entry, no doubt they had been reasonably close friends with the Stotesburys before their marriage in April 1749. Mary Stotesbury was the wife of Captain Edward Stotesbury. Charles and Sarah Wesley had visited often in their home, and brother John at times found their home a respite from his labors.

Charles's tribute to Mary Stotesbury is quite typical of a Christian spiritual life perspective in the eighteenth century: live a faithful life in Christ, look forward to a good death, and treasure the thoughts of life beyond death. In stanza 1, Charles states affirmatively that one cannot mourn her death, for in death she is "truly *born*" (1:7). Though there is an earthly birth, the unsurpassable true birth is in death, for one is born to eternal life with God.

Though she is dead, she is "followed by the works of love" (2:2) by those servants who saw her walk on earth and study how they might walk in her steps. That is quite a heritage, namely to

1. *MS Journal,* 2:595.

leave behind at death those who long to live and die the way Mary Stotesbury did.

In stanza 3, Charles enumerates aspects of her demeanor to be cherished and practiced by the faithful: calmness, steadfastness, faith, happiness, attentiveness, blamelessness, and peace.

Beginning in the last half of stanza 4, and continuing to the end of the poem, Charles places the lines within quotation marks, as if these are words Mary spoke before her death. They express her sense of God's pardoning grace and her confidence that Jesus Christ, the heavenly Lamb, has granted her life eternal. Her posture at death is one that Charles Wesley desires for all Christians:

> "Lo, I die, to meet my Love,
> Die, eternally to live." (6:7–8)

On the Death of Mrs. Mary Stotesbury
March 17, 1759[2]

1. Friendly, faithful soul, adieu,
     Joined to those escaped before!
   Thou hast gained the port in view,
     Thou hast reached the happy shore:
   Thee released we cannot mourn,
     Lightened of thine earthly load,
   Dead—or rather truly *born*,
     Dead to earth, thou livest to God.

2. Thou art gone to thy reward,
     Followed by the works of love,
   By the servants of thy Lord,
     All whose hearts are fixed above;
   Us, who saw thy walk below,
     Us, who seek thy place on high,
   Study in thy steps to go,
     Long like thee to live and die.

---

2. *FH* 1759, 16–18.

3. Calmly didst thou run thy race,
       Steadily thine end pursue;
    All the fruits of righteousness
       Proved thy faith divinely true:
    Happy thou for Christ prepared,
       Found, when all thy work was past,
    Watching to receive thy Lord,
       Blameless, and in peace at last.

4. Fruit of Jesu's lips and prayer,
       Peace thy parting soul attends;
    All thy dying words declare
       Life begun that never ends:
    "Blest be God, for ever blest,
       God of my salvation still!
    I am entered into rest,
       Pardon on my heart I feel.

5. What a gracious God is ours!
       How almighty to redeem!
    Blessings on his own he showers,
       Grace alone proceeds from him;
    He can only good ordain:
       This is life and death I prove,
    Happy I, though full of pain,
       Fuller still of joy and love.

6. "God for everything I praise,
       Every benefit divine,
    Chiefly for God's pardoning grace;
       Life, eternal life, is mine!
    Yes, I know, the heavenly Lamb,
       Whom I gladly die to see,
    He hath registered my name,
       Fitted up the house for me.

7. "Thither on *that 'pointed morn,*
        By God's Spirit signified,
    I shall to my Lord return,
        I God's pure, unspotted bride:
    Lo, the Bridegroom from above
        Comes my spirit to receive!
    Lo, I die, to meet my Love,
        Die, eternally to live."

CHAPTER 15

Miss M[olly] L[eysho]n

[d. April 12, 1750]

Based on two manuscript versions of this text, this is probably
Molly Leyshon, a cousin of Charles Wesley's wife, Sarah Gwynne.
Molly's mother was Mary Leyshon, born Gwynne (d. 1774), the
sister of Marmaduke Gwynne, Sarah Wesley's father. Molly is
mentioned twice in Charles's *MS Journal*.[1] The first entry speaks of
her as one of the participants in the Methodist movement, and the
second mentions that his wife Sarah was present in Ludlow when
Molly died on April 12, 1750. In any case, she was well-known to
Charles and Sarah, and she was a faithful member of the Methodist movement.

Unlike other death tributes of Charles, we do not learn much
about Molly Leyshon in this poem, especially as regards her relationship to others in service. But we do learn some things about
her. Apparently, she is someone who suffered, for in death "the
sense of misery" (2:5) is vanished:

> No pangs of loss or care
> Shall now thy bosom tear;
> Anguish and severe disease,
> Agony and death are past. (3:1–4)

1. *MS Journal*, 2:560, 593.

Molly is someone who has been "exposed to want and woe / By thine own flesh below," (5:1–2) but this is all now past. Because she is now at rest with her Redeemer, Charles does not mourn her passing. Rather he says,

> For ourselves, alas! we mourn,
> Still by various sorrows pained,
> Still by furious passions torn,
> 'Midst the toils of hell detained. (7:3–6)

Thus, he prays in concluding the poem:

> Come and take thy mourners up,
> Rank us with thy saints in light. (9:5–6)

There can be no question that Charles regards those of whom he writes as being ranked with God's "saints in light."

Thus, this poem, while a tribute to Molly Leyshon, does not concentrate so much on her person and witness, which is a characteristic of many of his lyrical death tributes. Here his emphasis is upon the hope we have in Christ, both now and beyond earthly life,[2] and the faithful preparation for a good death.

On the Death of M. L[eysho]n[3]
[April 12, 1750]

1.   Fly, happy spirit, fly
         Beyond this gloomy sky!
   Thee our prayers no more detain,
      Thee our grief recalls no more;
   Leave a while thy friends in pain,
      Land on that eternal shore.

2. See a similar poem with this emphasis, "On the Death of Mrs. Anne Davis," *PW*, 6:338–39. For another poem stressing preparation for a good death and hope beyond death, see "On the Death of Mrs. A[nne] C[owper]," *FH* 1746, 14–15.

3. *FH* 1759, 22–23.

2.   'Tis done, the soul is fled,
            The earthly part is dead!
      Dead is that which wished to die,
            That which galled the soul within,
      Dead the sense of misery,
            Dead the seed of death and sin.

3.   No pangs of loss or care
            Shall now thy bosom tear;
      Anguish and severe disease,
            Agony and death are past;
      Now the weary is at peace,
            Peace which shall for ever last.

4.   Yes, thou hast found an home
            Where want can never come:
      Nabal cannot drive thee thence,
            From thy bosom friends disjoin:
      Sure is that inheritance,
            Spite of hell for ever thine.

5.   Exposed to want and woe
            By thine own flesh *below,*
      Will thy relatives above
            Thee by their unkindness grieve?
      Angels cannot scorn thy love,
            God cannot his daughter leave.

6.   Thou *hast,* from earth conveyed,
            A place to lay thy head:
      Lulled on thy Redeemer's breast,
            We cannot lament for thee,
      Thee in God supremely blest,
            Blest through all eternity.

7. Yet on thy virgin-bier
      We drop a tender tear;
    For ourselves, alas! we mourn,
      Still by various sorrows pained,
    Still by furious passions torn,
      'Midst the toils of hell detained.

8. When, dearest soul, shall we
      Escape, and follow thee,
    Meekly bow our dying head,
      Gladly from our labor cease,
    Ready for the bridegroom made,
      Ripe for everlasting bliss?

9. Bridegroom of souls, reply,
      And bring redemption nigh;
    Object of our glorious hope,
      Come and change our faith to sight,
    Come and take thy mourners up,
      Rank us with thy saints in light.

CHAPTER 16

Miss F[rances] C[owper]

d. May 1742

Two sisters. Anne Cowper and Frances Cowper, daughters of William Cowper, Esq., of Enfield Chase near London, had poetical tributes dedicated to them by Charles Wesley. They were known to be friends with Selina, Countess of Huntingdon, having enjoyed the healing waters of Bath at the same time in February 1742. Thereafter, the two sisters went with the countess to her estate in Donington. Frances, for whom the poem below is written, became ill and died there in May 1742. How and when the Cowper sisters became friends with Charles Wesley is not known, but he may have met them through the Countess of Huntingdon. In any case, he knew them well enough to dedicate two poems to them on the occasion of their deaths.

We do not learn much about them personally from the poems (with the exception of Frances), which emphasize the importance of a faithful life ("Lived to only Christ below," 9:6), a good death ("O that at last even I, / Like thee might sweetly die," 14:1–2), and the joyous hope of heaven ("Taste the joys that never end," 15:6).

> O happy, happy soul,
> Thy heavenly joy is full! (13:1–2)

In the poem written for Frances or Fanny, however, Wesley provides more personal information than he does in the poem dedicated to Anne. In stanza 3, Wesley speaks of her demeanor, i.e., her "lamb-like innocence" (3:1). She bore the innocent likeness of Christ himself. He says that she was the "Closest follower of the Lamb" (9:6).

In her life of only twenty years she had been freed from the "infectious stain" of sin (3:5). She bore as well the "gentlest art" (5:1) of the Spirit to which her simple heart was opened, and like Lydia she believed "with ease" (5:6) in the sacrifice of Christ, "Him, thro' whom she all o'ercame" (9:4).

We learn further, in stanza 9, that she was a "Sharer of his richest grace" (9:5) and in stanza 10 that she was a woman of "spotless purity" (10:2).

With a short life so faithfully lived, it is not surprising that Wesley wells up with a cascade of praise for her, as a life ideal for all followers of Christ.

Hymn XII
On the Death of M[iss] F[rances/Fanny] C[owper][1]
[d. May 1742]

1. Thanks be to God alone
Thro' Jesus Christ his Son!
He who hath for all obtained,
Gives our friend the victory;
Sister, thou the prize hast gained,
Died for him who died for thee.

2. The mortal hour is past,
Thou hast o'ercome at last,
Freed from pain, for ever freed,
Ended is thy glorious strife,
Death, the latest foe, is dead,
Death is swallowed up of life.

1. *FH* 1746, 17–19; *PW,* 6:204–7. See also John Lampe's musical setting of this poem in *HGF* 1746, #24.

3. Thy lamb-like innocence
   Is soon departed hence,
From the world of sin and pain
   Thou art clean escaped away,
Saved from sin's infectious stain,
   Taken from the evil day.

4. Stranger to guilty fears
   Thou liv'dst thy twenty years,
From the great transgression free;
   Never did the poison spread,
Jesus, ere it rose in thee,
   Jesus crushed the serpent's head.

5. His Spirit's gentlest art
   Opened thy simple heart,
The eternal gospel-word,
   Lydia-like thou didst receive,
Fall before thy bleeding Lord,
   Own him, and with ease believe.

6. Soon as thy heart did feel
   The pardon-stamping seal,
Heard thy soul the warning cry,
   "Here thou hast not long to stay,
Rise, my love, make haste to die,
   Rise, my love, and come away!"

7. Thy cheerful soul obeyed,
   Thro' sufferings perfect made,
Perfect made in a short space,
   Thy resigned, and Christ-like soul,
Started forth, and won the race,
   Reached at once the glorious goal.

8. Aloft the spirit flies,
    And gains her native skies!
  Kindred souls salute her there,
    Springing from their azure throne,
  All in shouts their joy declare,
    All their new-born sister own.

9. Th' angelic army sings,
    And clap their golden wings!
  Harping with their harps they praise
    Him, thro' whom she all o'ercame,
  Sharer of his richest grace,
    Closest follower of the Lamb.

10. From love's soft witchcraft free
    Her spotless purity
  Lived to only Christ below;
    Higher now she reigns above,
  Mightier joys advanced to know,
    Honored with his choicest love.

11. Among the morning-stars
    A brighter crown she wears,
  With peculiar glories graced,
    Seated on a loftier throne,
  To superior raptures raised,
    Nearest God's eternal Son.

12. Mixt with the virgin-train
    She charms th' ethereal plain,
  With the Lamb for ever found;
    Angels listen while she sings,
  Catch th' inimitable sound,
    Music for the King of kings.

13. O happy, happy soul,
     Thy heavenly joy is full!
  Thee the Lamb hath made his bride,
     Called thee to his feast above,
  Thee he now hath glorified,
     Taught thee the new song of love.

14. O that at last even I,
     Like thee might sweetly die!
  Die, and leave a world of woe,
     Die out of the reach of sin,
  Die the joys of heaven to know;
     Open, Lord, and take me in!

15. Give me thy bliss to share,
     The meanest spirit there,
  Only let me see thy face,
     See with thee my happier friend,
  At an awful distance gaze,
     Taste the joys that never end.

16. Thou wilt cut short my years,
     And wipe away my tears:
  Lo! I wait thy leisure still,
     Humbly at thy footstool lie,
  Calm to suffer all thy will,
     Glad in thee to live and die.

CHAPTER 17

Prudence Box

d. January 9, 1778

As Charles Wesley notes, Prudence died at the age of thirty-eight.
Though deaths at this age in the eighteenth century were not un-
common, this struck indeed a disconcerting nerve for Charles's
family, for she had served them for a number of years in the 1770s
as a maid, and aided with the children, who were close to her. Her
difficult illness and extreme suffering must have grieved them.

The previous poem to Miss Molly L[eysho]n opens with an
extremely joyous line, "Fly, happy spirit, fly," with which Charles
celebrates the joyous outcome of life no longer burdened with
disease and misery. In the tribute to Prudence Box, however,
Charles dwells on the theme of suffering much more deliberately.
He implies that God does not take her to final victory in death, so
that she may linger in suffering and thus exhibit God's grace in the
midst of extreme sickness and pain. This is an interesting perspective, for it implies that God prolongs suffering.

> Lingering she drank the bitter cup
> Of grief and pain extreme. (2:5–6)

Why does this transpire? According to Wesley, it is because

> She languishes, in life detained,
> Superior grace to prove. (5:1–2)

Even though she has unquestionably confessed Christ the
crucified, and God hears her prayer for everlasting peace,

> Yet still her gracious Lord deferred
>> To sign her soul's release. (4:7–8)

She was obviously a woman of amazing strength, courage, and faith, overwhelmed with God's love in the face of death.

> She languishes, in life detained,
>> Superior grace to prove,
> Unshaken hope and faith unfeigned,
>> And all-victorious love.
> Love, heavenly love, her heart o'erflows,
>> Immense and unconfined
> To friends and relatives and foes
>> Embracing humankind. (5:1–8)

In her prayer, which Wesley uses to bring the poem to an end, she does not question her prolonged suffering and illness; rather she says: "I dare not murmur at thy stay" (7:5).

He ends her prayer with the hope that should be at the heart of every Christian's faith:

> "Into thy hands my soul receive,
>> That thee my soul may bless,
> May thee entirely love, and live
>> To thine eternal praise." (8:1–4)

> On the Death of Prudence Box
> January 9, 1778, aged thirty-eight[1]

> 1. God's come to set the prisoner free,
>> The dear Redeemer's come
> To give the final victory,
>> And take this servant home;
> To wipe the sorrow from her eyes,
>> To end her mourning days,
> And show her soul the glorious prize
>> In God's unclouded face.

---

1. *UP,* 3:327–29; *PW,* 6:339–41.

2. Long in the toils of death she lay,
   Nor feared the ghastly king,
   When Christ had borne her sins away,
   And spoiled him of his sting;
   Lingering she drank the bitter cup
   Of grief and pain extreme,
   And filled her after-passion[2] up,
   And *tasted* death with him.

3. Seeing the great Invisible,
   Her Savior and her Friend,
   She suffered all his righteous will,
   And suffered to the end:
   Through a long vale of misery,
   She walked with Christ her Guide,
   And bleeding on the hallowed tree,
   Confessed the Crucified.

4. With all the Spirit's powers she prayed,
   With infinite desire,
   To bow her weary, fainting head,
   And suddenly expire:
   The agonizing prayer was heard
   For everlasting peace;
   Yet still her gracious Lord deferred
   To sign her soul's release.

5. She languishes, in life detained,
   Superior grace to prove,
   Unshaken hope and faith unfeigned,
   And all-victorious love.
   Love, heavenly love, her heart o'erflows,
   Immense and unconfined
   To friends and relatives and foes
   Embracing humankind.

2. Cf. Col 1:24.

6. God holds her still in life detained,
    Her ripened grace to prove,
  Her steadfast hope and faith unfeigned,
    And all-victorious love:
To emulate God's sacrifice,
    Obtain a richer crown,
And point us to the opening skies,
    And pray the Savior down.

7. "Unutterable things I see!
    The purchase of thy blood,
The place he hath reserved for me!
    Come, O my God, my God!
I dare not murmur at thy stay;
    But to depart is best:
Come, O my Jesus, come away,
    And take me into rest!

8. "Into thy hands my soul receive,
    That thee my soul may bless,
May thee entirely love, and live
    To thine eternal praise."
She speaks, and hears the joyful word,
    "Come up, my spotless bride;"
And angels waft her to her Lord,
    And seat her at his side.

CHAPTER 18

Epitaphs

Three examples of epitaphs by Charles Wesley illustrate another form of lyrical expression through which he praises women for their exemplary faith and their stalwart and patient forbearance of pain and suffering.

Mrs. Susanna Wesley

The first epitaph for his mother, is a mini-autobiographical statement that telescopes her seventy years into twelve lines. At death, she exchanges the cross of seventy years' suffering for a crown. Here is found one of Charles's rare mentions in his poems in praise of eighteenth-century women of Holy Communion as a converting experience: "Him in the broken bread made known, / She knew, and felt her sins forgiven" (3:2–3). Furthermore, she died with the "lamb-like" posture of her Lord (4:4).

Epitaph of Susanna Wesley[1]

1. In sure and steadfast hope to rise,
   And claim her mansion in the skies,
   A Christian here her flesh laid down,
   The cross exchanging for the crown.

1. *HSP* 1749, 1:282, No. 172; *PW,* 5:86.

2. True daughter of affliction she,
   Inured to pain and misery,
   Mourned a long night of griefs and fears,
   A legal night of seventy years.

3. The Father then revealed his Son,
   Him in the broken bread made known,
   She knew, and felt her sins forgiven,
   And found the earnest of her heaven.

4. Meet for the fellowship above,
   She heard the call, "Arise, my love:"
   "I come," her dying looks replied,
   And lamb-like as her Lord she died!

Mrs. Eleanor Linnell

The two stanzas below on Mrs. Linnell constitute two epitaphs.

> The second "Adieu, dear Linnell!" is on the headstone of the grave of William Linnell in Brampton Old Church-yard, Cumberland. He was of Crow Hall and died on February 23, 1779, at age thirty-six, and served for a time as one of Wesley's preachers. The first . . . is for his wife Eleanor

but was probably composed before she died in 1791.[2]

As Charles remembers Mrs. Linnell, he once again uses the "Martha-Mary Formula"—Martha's good care, Mary's better part—and adds Lydia's open heart, emphasizing the example of how one should live. However, in praising Mrs. Linnell, he adds two other biblical women whose examples should be followed! The "virtuous wife with Rachel's comely face" and Sarah's (Abraham's wife) obedience. Here one sees Charles's poetical gift of eloquent English diction which integrates characteristics of five women

---

2. See *UP* 3:325n2.

of Holy Scripture, all exemplified in the life of one woman: Mrs. Linnell.

> Epitaph to Mrs. Linnell of Whittlebury
> Then of Brampton, Cumb[erland]

1. This silent grave, it doth embrace
   A virtuous wife with Rachel's comely face,
   Sarah's obedience, Lydia's open heart,
   Martha's good care, and Mary's better part.

2. Adieu! dear Linnell! from the shades of night
   Thy passage swift into the realms of light.
   Hard was thy conflict, but thy pains are o'er
   And trouble never shall oppress thee more.

Mary Horton

Wesley's poem "On the Death of Mary Horton," which is addressed above, contains thirty-five stanzas of six lines each and is divided into five parts. In the epitaph for her he cannot capture all of the aspects of her life that he has rehearsed in that lengthy poem. Nevertheless, in the epitaph below of six lines he encapsulates the hallmarks of her obedient and faithful life: meekness, humility, salvation in Christ, purity, blameless pilgrimage with Christ, being filled with love, and the discovery of eternal rest with God.

> Epitaph [For Mary Horton][3]

> A meek and lowly Follower of the Lamb,
> She more than conquered all in Jesus' name,
> Washed in his blood, and kept her garments white,
> And blameless walked in her Redeemer's sight,
> Till filled with Love she fainted on his breast,
> And found within his arms her everlasting Rest!

3. Published posthumously in *PW*, 8:437 and *RV*, 374–75.

Section 3

Prose

CHAPTER 19

A Short Account
of the Death of Hannah Richardson

After the study of some of the poems of Charles Wesley regarding
women of the Bible and eighteenth-century women whom he lifts
up to the church and world at large as the highest examples of how
to live the Christian faith, it is important to examine the lengthiest
prose document (eleven pages) he composed about the death of an
individual, namely Hannah Richardson.[1] To be sure, he has dealt
with the faith struggles of some women in his lyrical accounts of
their lives and deaths. And he often places a strong emphasis on "a
good death." In the case of Hannah Richardson, however, Charles
dwells in detail on the agonizing struggle of a follower of Christ to
find the assurance of faith and its discovery immediately prior to
death.

His account of Hannah's death is written very much like a
pastoral verbatim report from the time he first called on her,
through the desperate struggle to find ultimate assurance in
Christ, and its final discovery. His first journal entry regarding
Hannah is on April 18, 1741: "Called to one that was dying. It was
Hannah Richardson."[2] His experience with her and her ultimate
faith triumph are so important to him that on occasion he reads

1. Wesley, *A Short Account of the Death.*

2. *MS Journal,* 1:298.

portions of his account of her death to Methodist Society members when they gather.

> Sunday, May 31. . . Read in the Society my account of Hannah Richardson's death. She, being dead, yet spoke so powerfully to our hearts that my voice was lost in sorrowful sighing of such as be in captivity. To several God showed himself the God of consolation also, particularly to two young Welshmen whom his providence sent hither from Carmarthen. They had heard most dreadful stories of us—Arminians, freewillers, perfectionists, Papists—which all vanished like smoke when they came to hear with their own ears. God applied to their hearts the word of his power. I carried them to my lodgings and stocked them with books, and sent them away, recommended to the grace of God which bringeth salvation unto all men.[3]

Hannah's experience of suffering and agony in the quest for full assurance in Christ becomes for Charles a barometer by which he measures the same in the lives of others. For example, on June 17, 1741, he records in his *MS Journal*:

> Gave the Sacrament to our sister Brimble, dying in such strong agony as I have not seen before, no not in Hannah Richardson. She had no fear of hell, yet was so deeply convinced of original sin, as made all who heard her tremble. She could not let go her confidence that God would finish his work in her, though there were so few hours between her and eternity.[4]

Charles opens his account of Hannah Richardson by explaining that she was a woman of "sorrowful spirit," though she had been awakened by God from a young age and sought "to establish her own righteousness, seeking acceptance (as we did all) not by faith, but as it were by the works of the law."[5] Hence, this is Charles's beginning point of her quest: it is well meaning, but has the wrong

---

3. *MS Journal*, 1:311.

4. *MS Journal*, 1:314.

5. Wesley, *A Short Account of the Death*, 3.

goal. He describes her as one who gave faithful attention to God's word, but received no benefit from it. How well he knew about that from his own experience. It was as if in her quest she would say, "Behold, I go forward, but [God] is not there, and backward, but I cannot perceive Him; on the left-hand, where he doth work, but I cannot behold Him."[6]

Charles speaks of her self-image: she could not think one good thought, distracted with doubts and fears, despaired of life itself, mourned all day long, and refused to be comforted. Yet she would not give up, for a "spark of hope lay as at the very bottom of her heart."[7] Charles seemed truly amazed at her persistence in struggle and confessed: "I am a witness to her many complaints and wailings. Yet she persisted with a glorious obstinacy."[8]

According to Charles, there is a pattern in the experience of Hannah Richardson for the seekers of ultimate truth: persist, persist, persist! And he speaks as well of her exemplary social demeanor amid all her agony and turmoil: "She was exceeding tender hearted towards the sick, whether in body or soul."[9] Charles's advice to others who would follow Hannah's example is found in Luke 10:37, which he quotes thusly: "Go thou and do likewise."

Even though she persisted, Charles goes to visit her and finds her in utter despair. How is it possible that one so sincerely seeks to find full assurance of faith in Christ and it does not transpire? He knows this is the experience of many. There is a subtle emphasis on the value of routine in the practice of piety in Charles's account of Hannah's quest, for he lets it be known that Hannah was a woman faithful in the study of the word, in prayer, and in attendance at Holy Communion, even when these things seemed to mean nothing. "She waited in a constant use of all the means of grace; never missed the Communion, or hearing the Word, tho' all was torment to her, for she never found benefit."[10]

6. Wesley, *A Short Account of the Death*, 4.
7. Wesley, *A Short Account of the Death*, 5.
8. Wesley, *A Short Account of the Death*, 5.
9. Wesley, *A Short Account of the Death*, 5.
10. Wesley, *A Short Account of the Death*, 5.

In Charles's record of at least five visits with Hannah, there appears to be a back-and-forth between doubt and faith before she finally declares: "Liberty! Liberty! This is the glorious liberty of the sons of God! I know it, I see it, I feel it. Believe, believe there is such a liberty! and he will give it you. I am sanctified, wholly, spirit, soul and body. . . I am made perfect in love."[11]

As Charles concludes his story of Hannah's persistence and victory, he also includes the account of her witness to one of her sisters, who in her doubt was comforted by the Holy Spirit. Of this moment Charles says, "O how sweetly did she lament over her! I never saw such sympathy! The Spirit in her mourned like a Turtle-dove, and made intercession with groanings that cannot be uttered."[12]

Hannah's was the "good death" of which Charles had so often spoken: "She went away without any agony, or sigh, or groan. She only rested; and sweetly fell asleep in the arms of Jesus."[13]

---

11. Wesley, *A Short Account of the Death*, 8, 10.

12. Wesley, *A Short Account of the Death*, 10.

13. Wesley, *A Short Account of the Death*, 11.

Summary

1. Roles of Women

What may we conclude in summary about the women of whom Charles Wesley speaks in his lyrical tributes? Though there were no women priests in the Church of England in the eighteenth century, some of the roles Charles attributes to them are certainly a part of the priestly office.

They fulfill a *kerygmatic* role in that they proclaim the gospel, hoping to lead others to Christ and the church. And yet, often this *kerygmatic* role does not involve words, for they proclaim the gospel by the very act of being and doing. Mary Magdalene is the first to proclaim the good news at the time of the resurrection of Jesus. She also fulfills a *didactic* role, for she teaches the apostles of the Lamb.

Women, according to Charles Wesley, also fulfill the role of doing works of righteousness in both secular and sacred arenas. Mary Naylor, for example, was a "nursing mother to the poor" and sought justice for all.

Many of the women of whom Charles writes fulfill the role of humble servants. In contrast to an eighteenth-century world that barred them from education and just employment, one by one, these women serve humbly in diverse menial roles in English society.

2. Nature or Character of Women

How does Charles Wesley define the character of the women of whom he writes? They are grace-filled women, i.e., in all dimensions of their lives they are ruled by grace. This results in active and patient faith. They are compassionate and have a reservoir of strength for the poor.

In their sympathy, compassion, and ability to feel the needs of others, they are examples of the best aspects of an eighteenth-century "culture of sensibility."[1]

They are social human beings marked by sacred, social character and formed by social love. There is a constancy and transparency about them which is seen in openness and friendship. Even amid life's most difficult moments of agony and despair, they do not forget their social character and the need of social love—they remember to care of others.

3. Goals and Purpose of These Women

Charles Wesley does not leave us guessing as to the goals and purpose of these women's lives. They are here on earth to do the will of God, and to pursue the patient love of Christ with eagerness and composure. They bear the burdens of those who disown Christ, and pray for them. These are women who lead a life of prayer and commune with Christ and the church. Nevertheless, theirs is not a passive faith. They are engaged in social service, pursuing justice at all costs. This means that their stewardship of gifts and resources must be just.

They show mercy to all, especially those in distress. In so doing, they personify a redeemed and holy life. They grow in wisdom and insight and are cheerfully obedient, seeing God in common tasks and simple things. Through it all, as followers of Christ, they prepare to live and they prepare to die.

1. See page xviii of this book.

4. Importance for the Wesleyan Movement

What is the importance of these women for the Wesleyan movement, and indeed for the church as a whole? They model the life of faith for followers of Christ. They are personifications of what John Wesley speaks of as "practical divinity." They reveal self-effacing, active faith, and wise counsel. Thus, they provide a vision of what life sustained by God's revelation in Christ really means in everyday life.

According to Charles, many of these women have a very realistic view of human nature, and often they illustrate the wedding of mind, heart, and hands better than many men of eighteenth-century England who claim to be followers of Christ. They seek a balance between active faith and the contemplative life.

5. Key Attitudes Revealed in These Women

There are three key attitudes of these women that serve the church and humankind well in every age:

(1) The attitude toward the Christian life: seek wisdom, always seek peace, be diligent in studying God's word, and become like the meek Spirit of Christ.

(2) The attitude toward others: always be formed for love and friendship, and live for others that their lives may be reclaimed for and by God.

(3) The positive attitude toward death: welcome death in Jesus' name—the *only* life posture for living, whether in good health or illness. In facing death, bear grief with integrity, confidence, and assurance.

If followed, the ways in which Charles Wesley allows these women to speak to us in the above five categories will revolutionize the message and action of churches which are diminishing in growth and influence in a twenty-first-century world.

Selected Bibliography

"An Account of Hannah Harrison." *MM* 25 (1802) 318–23.

"An Account of Mrs. Crosby, of Leeds." *MM* 29 (1806) 418–23.

"An Account of Mrs. Sarah Ryan." *AM* 2 (1779) 296–310.

"An Extract from the Diary of Mrs. Bathsheba Hall." *AM* 4 (1781) 35–40, 94–97, 148–52, 195–98, 256–59, 309–11, 372–75.

Barker, Esther T. *Lady Huntingdon, Whitefield and the Wesleys*. Maryville, TN: E. T. Barker, 1984.

Brown, Earl Kent. *Women of Mr Wesley's Methodism*. New York: Edwin Mellen, 1983.

Burham, Elizabeth. "Susanna Wesley's Influence Upon the Hymnody of Her Sons." *Methodist Review* 112 (1929) 540–50.

Chilcote, Paul Wesley. "Charles Wesley and Christian Practices." *Proceedings of The Charles Wesley Society* 12 (2008) 35–47.

———. *John Wesley and the Women Preachers of Early Methodism*. London: Scarecrow, 1991.

———. "Songs of the Heart." *Proceedings of The Charles Wesley Society* 5 (1998) 99–114.

Cole, Joseph, ed. *Memoir of Hannah Ball*. Revised and enlarged by John Parker. London: J. Mason, 1839.

Cruickshank, Joanna. "'The Suffering Members Sympathise': Constructing the Sympathetic Self in the Hymns of Charles Wesley." In *Charles Wesley Life, Literature and Legacy*, edited by Kenneth G. C. Newport and Ted A. Campbell, 245–63. Peterborough, UK: Epworth, 2007.

Dallimore, Arnold A. *Susanna: The Mother of John and Charles Wesley*. Darlington, UK: Evangelical, 1992.

Edwards, Maldwyn L. *Dear Sister: The Story of John Wesley and Women in His Life*. London: Epworth, 1959.

"The Experience of Mrs. Ann Gilbert." *AM* 18 (1795) 42–46.

Lloyd, Gareth. "Sarah Perrin (1721–1787) — Early Methodist Exhorter." *Methodist History* 41 (2002) 79–88.

Ludwig, Charles. *Susanna Wesley: Mother of John and Charles*. Millford, MI: Mott Media, 1984.

McMullen, Michael D., ed. *Hearts Aflame: Prayers of Susanna, John and Charles Wesley*. London: Triangle, 1995.

Moore, Henry. *The Life of Mrs Mary Fletcher*. Birmingham, UK: J. Peart, 1817.

Newton, John. *Susanna Wesley and the Puritan Tradition in Methodism*. Revised edition. Peterborough, UK: Epworth, 2002.

Pipe, John. "Memoir of Miss Isabella Wilson." *MM* 31 (1808) 372–75, 410–15, 461–69, 516–18, 562–67, 595–97.

Quantrille, Wilma J. "A Woman Responds to Charles Wesley." *Methodist History* (1991) 199–212.

Rogers, Hester Ann. *An Account of the Experience of Hester Ann Rogers*. London: Methodist Conference office, 1794.

Stokes, Mary. "The Experience of Miss Mary Stokes." *AM* 18 (1795) 99–101.

Wallace, Charles. "'Some State Employment of Your Mind': Reading, Writing, and Religion in the Life of Susanna Wesley." *Church History* 58 (1989) 354–66.

Wallace, Charles, ed. *Susanna Wesley: The Complete Writings*. New York: Oxford University Press, 1997.

Wesley, Charles. *Letters upon Sacred Subjects, By a Person [Mrs. Lefevre] Lately Deceased*. London: n.p, 1757.

———. *MS Acts*. http://divinity.duke.edu/sites/divinity.duke.edu/files/documents/cswt/75_MS_Acts.pdf.

———. *MS Death of Mary Horton*. http://divinity.duke.edu/sites/divinity.duke.edu/files/documents/cswt/47_MS_Death_of_Mary_Horton.pdf.

———. *MS Funeral Hymns*. http://divinity.duke.edu/sites/divinity.duke.edu/files/documents/cswt/35_MS_Funeral_Hymns_1756-87.pdf.

———. *MS Luke*. http://divinity.duke.edu/sites/divinity.duke.edu/files/documents/cswt/78_MS_Luke.pdf.

———. "On Being Desired to Write an Elegy for Mrs Hannah Butts." *CSWT*, 32–33.

———. "On the Death of Mrs. A[nne] C[owper]." *FH* 1746, 14–15.

———. "On the Death of Mrs. Anne Davis." *PW*, 6:338–39.

———. "On the Death of Mrs. Hannah Butts." *CSWT*, 33–41.

———. *A Short Account of the Death of Mrs. Hannah Richardson*. Bristol, UK: Farley, 1741.

Index of Personal Names